Zakariyya Tamir and the Politics of the Syrian Short Story

Zakariyya Tamir and the Politics of the Syrian Short Story

Modernity, Authority and Gender

Alessandro Columbu

I.B.TAURIS
LONDON • NEW YORK • OXFORD • NEW DELHI • SYDNEY

I.B. TAURIS
Bloomsbury Publishing Plc
50 Bedford Square, London, WC1B 3DP, UK
1385 Broadway, New York, NY 10018, USA
29 Earlsfort Terrace, Dublin 2, Ireland

BLOOMSBURY, I.B. TAURIS and the I.B. Tauris logo are trademarks of
Bloomsbury Publishing Plc

First published in Great Britain 2023
This paperback edition published 2024

Series design by Adriana Brioso
Cover image © Carlos Spottorno/Panos Pictures

A catalogue record for this book is available from the British Library.

A catalog record for this book is available from the Library of Congress.

ISBN: HB: 978-0-7556-4413-1
PB: 978-0-7556-4409-4
ePDF: 978-0-7556-4412-4
eBook: 978-0-7556-4411-7

Typeset by Deanta Global Publishing Services, Chennai, India

Contents

Introduction 1

1 From commitment to exile: Zakariyya Tamir, the forefather of the modern Syrian short story 15

2 Changing masculinity: *Ḥadātha*, nationalism and authoritarianism in the 1960s and 1970s 39

3 The modern female: Female sexuality in the stories of the '*ḥadāthī*' period until the 1970s 59

4 From object to subject: Multiplicity, transgression and the sexualization of the female 79

5 The fall of the strong man: Virility, homosexuality and the *qabaday* 99

Conclusion 117

Appendix 123

Notes 136

Bibliography 151

Index 159

Introduction

The intimate relationship between modern Arabic literature and the socio-political developments in the Middle East has been widely addressed and it is uncommon to come across studies that overlook the tight bonds between contemporary literature in Arabic and the historical events in the region.[1] In Syria literature, political trends and historical developments have been intimately connected and inseparable, to the extent that some consider this relationship and the way politics and history reverberate in novels, plays and short stories the main trait that characterizes Syrian literature.[2] However, while cultural production from other countries in the region such as Egypt and Palestine has received considerable attention from European and North American academia, Syrian literature was until very recently a generally unexplored subject and a relative scantiness of resources was the norm.[3]

This work aims at filling this void in the study of contemporary Arabic and Syrian literature by analysing the works of the Syrian Zakariyya Tamir (b. 1931, from now on Tamir), an author widely considered the forefather of the modern short story in Syria, as well as an innovator in terms of both style and content in the broader field of Arabic literature.[4] Born in Damascus in 1931, Tamir is one of the most significant figures in the contemporary literary scene of Syria and the wider Middle East. This study addresses his literary trajectory by situating the stylistic and thematic transformations his works have undergone in the context of major historical and political events in Syria. Moreover, it explores the stylistic and thematic transformations of Tamir's works in the context of a process of political and ideological fragmentation affecting Syria and the wider Arab East since the mid-1970s. This book examines also the peculiarities of the short story as a literary genre in this writer's works, as well as the significance of literary commitment, masculinity, patriarchy, sexuality and female identity in relation to nationalism, modernization and authoritarianism.

The suggestive, politicized and politically committed nature of this author's oeuvre is widely acknowledged; however, the implications of a style that denounces authoritarian violence and oppression have not been addressed from the point of view of gender studies. This book addresses the multiple configurations that the male and female protagonists of Tamir's stories have assumed throughout his career to reveal their conformity or subversion to a patriarchal conceptualization of gender roles. This study seeks to explain the advantages and limitations of a style that makes extensive use of bodily and sexual connotations, simultaneously transforming and reinforcing normative conceptualizations of gender identities, exposing unconcealed sexual desire, breaking certain taboos, and emphasizing others. In particular, the focus is on representations that tackle or reinforce masculinity and femininity as performing two strict, separate and polarized subjectivities.

This work looks at the short stories of Tamir as works of art whose multiple dimensions, collective and political, individual and atypical, male and female, reflect the specificity of Syria's experiences of modernization, nationalism, authoritarian rule, defeat, occupation and ideological fragmentation in the latter half of the twentieth century. Employing a theoretical approach to the study of fiction and its social dimension that can be loosely defined as Marxist, but in its multiple and diverse configurations,[5] this book examines the relationship between the formal transformations that Tamir's short stories have undergone and the ways in which representations of masculinity and femininity have evolved in relation to historical events. In this vein, this study explains these transformations in style and content as signalling a slowly but steadily changing worldview and a declining nationalist ideology, not as a separate superstructure detached from consciousness and relationships but rather as social experience that is interrelated with 'structures of feelings' concerning the lived experience of men and women. This study looks at the form and content of Tamir's works throughout his career as intimately interconnected, giving consideration to the way the form of Tamir's stories, their structure and style have been historically determined by the content they have embodied. The analysis connects the linguistic and strictly literary features of Tamir's short stories with changing representations of gender roles and their implications in relation to nationalism, patriarchy and authoritarianism.

In his analysis of the relationship between the major political transformations and cultural production in the Arab Middle East since the 1970s, the Syrian literary critic Kamal Abu Deeb brings together the decline of emancipatory ideologies that dominated the political landscape after the 1940s on the one hand, and newly emergent literary modes of expression that have blossomed across the region on the other.[6] Central to Abu Deeb's argument is the detailed account of two trends of literary production in Arabic which emerged in different historical conditions: the first – called modernist, or *ḥadāthī* (from the Arabic *ḥadātha*, for modernity) – being organic to nationalist, socialist and emancipatory ideologies; the second, exemplified by a number of works showcasing the crisis of ideology and authority, which began in the early 1970s until today. The trends in Arabic literature in the decades between the 1980s and 2000s have been interpreted by Abu Deeb as the result of a process of fragmentation on a political and ideological level, and as the consequence of the collapse of the totalizing discourse of modernity (*ḥadātha*). Up until the 1970s cultural creation had derived its vitality from a collective project whose failure and collapse have engendered a variety of new styles and themes, including a shift to a female viewpoint in the focus on specifically feminist issues.[7]

Although Abu Deeb does not make mention of Tamir's short stories in his essays, this author's oeuvre exemplifies some of the radical transformations that the collapse of totalizing discourse has brought about in contemporary Arabic literature. Tamir's early collections of short stories first appeared at a point in history in which the influence and impact of nationalism and socialism on cultural production was at its peak. The rest of his works on the other hand appeared between the 1970s and 2000s, the three decades during which the transformations Abu Deeb analyses have manifested more significantly. Abu Deeb offers two different ways of theorizing this process and its effects on cultural production, either as a fragmentation of all concepts of unity and singularity or alternatively as a breeding ground for the emergence of a variety of voices and points of view. The fragmented and apparently uncommitted nature of Tamir's writing – first detectable in his 1970s works – has brought about transformations and a proliferation of themes and voices, with new configurations for femininity and masculinity which subvert a patriarchal worldview on gender roles, desire and sexuality.

Throughout the five chapters, the book explores Tamir's short stories following a theme-based chronological approach to the evolution of their style and content. The first three chapters deal with Tamir's early works published between the late 1950s and early 1980s putting them in conversation with the preeminent literary and political trends in Syria and the wider Middle East, as well as the impact of the experiences of independence, modernization, war, occupation and dispossession. This part explores the organic relationship Arabic literature enjoyed with the project of national liberation as well as the progressive and existentialist struggle for emancipation from authoritarianism, patriarchy, religious tradition and exploitation. The last two chapters, devoted to the analysis of Tamir's latest works, look more closely at the political significance of prominent female characters openly expressing their sexual desire, simultaneously assessing their subjectivity and acting as decisive actors that shape the male protagonists' masculinity.

Chapter 1 outlines the elements of novelty and originality of Tamir's early stories against the background of the predominant literary trends in Syria and the Arab East to situate Tamir as a *committed* writer as understood by his generation of writers of fiction. The chapter draws on relevant examples from the debates taking place in Syrian literary magazines in the 1960s and 1970s to investigate the committed nature of Tamir's work and its evolution in parallel (and often in contrast) with the main trends of the Syrian and Arab literary field. The chapter then goes on to introduce the works of Tamir's later period and their main stylistic transformations as compared to the stories of his early period. This part addresses the style and the literary strategies that characterize the works of this period in the context of the persistent rule of an authoritarian regime and its increased presence in the life of citizens and intellectuals. In this context the themes of exile, diaspora and revolution play a crucial role to ascertain the new forms of political engagement that have emerged in his writing and in Syrian and Arabic literature in general. For this purpose, the events of the Syrian revolution come into the picture to clarify the significance of Tamir's symbolic participation in the 2011 uprising against the Assad regime.

The second and third chapters deal with Tamir's first five collections which appeared between 1960 and 1978 – *Ṣahīl al-jawād al-abyaḍ* (The neighing of the white steed),[8] *Rabīʿ fī al-ramād* (Spring in the ashes),[9] *al-Raʿd* (The thunder),[10] *Dimashq al- ḥarāʾiq* (Damascus of fires)[11] and *al-Numūr fī al-yawm al-ʿāshir* (Tigers on the tenth day)[12] – investigating the ways in which a predominantly modernist, anti-patriarchal and emancipatory ideological tone was reflected in the form of the stories as well as in the roles performed by male and female characters. The five collections are subjected to an analysis of different configurations of gender roles, which brings into view the relationship between the modernist character of the first works, the changing representations of male and female protagonists and their underlying conceptualization of sexuality. The analysis looks at ideology and commitment as reflected in Tamir's representations of male and female characters and at the impact of modernism in the form and structure of the short stories in this period, examining the roles usually assigned to male and female protagonists and the specific ideological stance they channel. In addition, the second and third chapters address the extent to which these predominantly modernist and ideological influences gradually changed in Tamir's works since the early 1970s and the ways this was reflected in both the form and the content of the stories published between 1970 and 1978. Moreover, these chapters address the implications of sexuality, the body and the different connotations attached to female and male protagonists in stories that denounce the asphyxiating nature of the patriarchal family as an allegory for authoritarian oppression and control.

Finally, the last two chapters focus on the works published by Tamir between 1994 and 2002: *Nidā' Nūḥ* (Noah's summon),[13] *Sa-naḍḥak* (We shall laugh),[14] *al-Ḥiṣrim* (Sour grapes),[15] *Taksīr Rukab* (Breaking knees).[16] The fourth chapter takes the analysis further, to examine differences and commonalities in the representations of female sexuality between Tamir's early and later stories. This part elucidates the political dimension of a more equal approach to the sexes and the transgressive representations of female sexuality in Tamir's latest work, with a focus on female performances of sexuality under the rule of an authoritarian albeit supposedly progressive regime. The analysis of stories concerning female sexuality addresses the extent to which the development of these representations throughout Tamir's career contradicts or is an indication or even an anticipation of the retreat of progressive nationalist ideologies and the changes witnessed in the field of cultural production. Feminine and masculine identities as mutually informed underpin this study, hence the fifth and final chapter closes the circle by returning to the study of male characters, seeking to determine the extent to which the emergence of strong and omnipresent female characters has affected the representations of male protagonists. The last chapter examines the transformations that the most recurrent representations of masculinity in Tamir's later stories display in the context of ideological and political fragmentation. Moreover, the chapter looks at how the multiplicity of voices and themes brought about by the process of fragmentation challenges a polarized notion of gender roles.

The decision to divide this author's oeuvre into two periods is motivated by the disparity between the historical periods in which different collections appeared. Most studies of contemporary Arabic and Syrian literature that connect aesthetic and thematic transformations to historical events pinpoint their chronological demarcation between the pre- and post-1967 writings.[17] Undoubtedly, in a field with such robust bonds with the Arab nationalist cause as contemporary Arabic literature was in the 1960s, no author or critic could have possibly been indifferent to events of such magnitude and long-lasting impact as the Six Days War. Yet, on closer inspection, Tamir's stories cannot easily be grouped in the same fashion. For this purpose it is important to point out the fundamental role local literary magazines played in showcasing young writers as an important aspect of Syria's literary market that some of the most important contributions on Tamir's work have overlooked.[18] The role of magazines such *al-Ādāb* or *Shiʿr* for cultural debate in the Arab East can hardly be overstated, and it was precisely in the pages of such outlets that Tamir made his first appearance as a young writer on the Arab literary scene. By the time his first compilation of short stories (*Ṣahīl al-jawād al-abyaḍ*) appeared in 1960 all the stories contained in it had appeared at different times between 1958 and 1959 in *al-Ādāb* and other magazines, printed mostly in Damascus and Beirut. The publication of *Rabīʿ fī al-ramād* in 1963 followed a similar pattern: out of eleven stories, seven had previously been published between 1960 and 1962 in a variety of Syrian, Lebanese and Egyptian magazines. The same is also true for some of the stories from *al-Raʿd*, which appeared in 1970 and whose stories were published by the Arab Writers' Union official periodical *al-Maʿrifa* between 1967 and 1969. Closely aligning publishing dates with concurrent historical events is particularly problematic in *Dimashq al-ḥarāʾiq*, which was published in 1973 but contains stories that appeared as early as 1960 in *al-Ādāb*, displaying developments and transformations that cannot be clearly situated in the context of the post-1967 defeat.

Overlooking this peculiarity of the literary market in Syria inevitably leads to overgeneralization and cause-effect explanations charged with fallacy and inaccuracy, and the impact of historical events – important as they may have been – must not be overstated. Considering that Tamir started writing and publishing short stories in literary magazines as early as 1958 this aspect attains greater criticality with the collections published in the 1970s, because the time span between the date of publication of the original stories and that of the individual collections becomes much wider. The historical and political context in which such stories, in their form and content, were imagined, produced and negotiated must not be inferred simply from the individual collections' date of publication. (See Appendix 1.1.)

The second period of Tamir's oeuvre, on the other hand, marks further fundamental formal transformations that also substantiate the choice to divide his works into two separate periods. Thirteen years of literary 'silence' followed Tamir's relocation to the UK in 1981, during which he did not publish any collections of short stories. The collections published from his self-imposed exile to England contain only original stories that have not appeared in any other literary outlet and are distinguished from his earlier works for a greater deal of homogeneity in the themes addressed. While, for example, *Nidā' Nūḥ* and *Sa-naḍḥak* have a more manifest focus on Arab historical tradition in contrast with a present typified by pessimism, in *al-Ḥiṣrim* and *Taksīr Rukab* the role of sexuality and the changing nature of masculinity emerges more prominently.

While much has been written about the emergence of female Arab authors and their representations of female characters and their sexuality in Arabic literature, the exploration of masculinities with regard to concurrent historical circumstances has remained a relatively unexplored subject.[19] The distancing of Arabic cultural production from a traditional form of commitment to the causes of modernization and national liberation has not resulted in an unambiguous separation between fiction and politics. In turn, the persistence of authoritarianism has reshaped the political dimension of cultural production, particularly with regard to gender roles and sexuality.[20] The greater presence of sexual images in Syrian and Arabic literature since the 1970s allows us to situate the transformation of Tamir's style within a trend that has affected cultural production from the Arab East extensively, but whose implications and significance remain relatively understudied. While the relevance of the transgressive representations of female sexual desire can be safely interpreted as an attack against a patriarchal worldview that disapproves of women expressing their sexual desire openly, gender roles seen from the point of view of men have further implications.

For this purpose, the study of gender roles and representations of masculinities and femininities as mutually informed conceptualizations and its application to contemporary Arabic literature represents a crucial reference point. The concept of hegemonic masculinity proposed by R. W. Connell provides the theoretical framework to approach the changing representations of gender roles in relation to the historical and political context,[21] and questions the social, political and cultural dynamics that underpin patriarchy, that is, the 'dominant position of men and the subordination of women'.[22] The model of hegemonic masculinity represents a normative way of performing one's masculinity that reinforces men's superiority in society. Far from normatively presenting men as a monolithic social group Connell's studies examine patriarchy and the privilege that men derive from it through a variety of categories including hegemonic, complicit, marginal and subordinate masculinities, stressing possible transitions from one dominant position to another. Borrowing from Gramsci's interpretation of class relations, Connell defines *hegemonic* masculinity as the configuration of gender practice that embodies the currently accepted answer to the problem of the legitimacy of patriarchy. Connell's theory explains *complicit* forms of masculinity affiliated with non-overtly dominant practices which nevertheless reinforce patriarchy by indifferently accepting the existing organization of gender roles, although they do not entail openly misogynist behaviours.[23] In addition, Connell notes that *subordinate* masculinity reinforces hegemonic masculinities through seemingly transgressive performances which nevertheless throw normative understandings of gender roles into relief. Besides, the concept of subordinate masculinity introduces the idea that hegemonic masculinity performs its dominant position through men in relation to women, but also onto other *men*.[24]

This study situates Tamir's works also in a specifically Syrian context and their aesthetic transformations within the framework of Syrian literature, a field that has developed a set of themes that have become 'typical', and mostly ascribable to the nature of the authoritarian regime that has dominated its political life since the 1970s.[25] This peculiarly local character becomes relevant in the light of three further subcategories that Connell's theory of masculinity puts forward. While initially framing hegemonic masculinity as based on 'the global dominance of men over women',[26] in its most recent version the theory considers masculinities at three different levels, namely, the local, the regional and the global:

1. Local: constructed in the arenas of face-to-face interaction of families, organizations, and immediate communities, as typically found in ethnographic and life-history research;
2. Regional: constructed at the level of the culture or the nation-state, as typically found in discursive, political and demographic research;
3. Global: constructed in transnational arenas such as world politics and transnational business and media, as studied in the emerging research on masculinities and globalization.[27]

Particularly in its local and regional configurations the concept of hegemonic masculinity becomes relevant to the Syrian context that is the object of this analysis. Looking at the interaction of these two levels, Connell highlights the intimate connection and mutually informed nature of local (familial) and regional (national) patriarchy, adding to the argument proposed by Hisham Sharabi and Halim Barakat about twentieth-century authoritarianism as an intensification of patriarchy, linking the rise of authoritarianism-cum-patriarchy to the failed projects of modernization. According to Sharabi, common to most regimes in the region is 'the transideological model of authority'[28] and the employment of a patriarchal discourse that served to reinforce authoritarianism as the unquestionable provider of unity and harmony. On the other hand, Barakat's analysis of the Arab contemporary family situated the most widespread patterns of familial structures at the intersection between politics and religious beliefs, arguing that authoritarianism derives its legitimacy from the widespread organization of the family as male-centred. In particular, Barakat emphasized the role of the patriarchal family as the primary source of identification and political orientation for the individual, shaped by the dominant figure of the father, whose dominance reproduces the same rituals and coercion typical of authoritarianism.[29]

The Assad regime in Syria has employed familial metaphors extensively to construct a cult of the leader that functions as the source of identification for all Syrians and demands loyalty from his children-citizens in exchange for protection.[30] This rhetoric in turn is based on traditional icons of loving, austere fathers as the centre of families, and on widespread standards of family that are patriarchal and pyramidally hierarchical. Lisa Wedeen has analysed in detail the semiotic implications of the ideological representations of Syria as the metaphorical family in connection with political atomization and authoritarianism under the Assad regime.[31] Wedeen shows how this transposition of the familial into the national in contemporary Syria has been constructed in peculiar ways so as to reinforce obedience without necessarily eliciting genuine veneration for the supreme figure of the dictator. By emphasizing the harmonious and fraternal nature of public life in Syria, the state narrative stresses the centrality of the patriarchal family as 'natural', and of the father as the benevolent and wise leader of his children. The two levels of familial and national identification processes are intertwined in a narrative that appropriates the existing patterns of familial loyalty and obedience, projecting them onto the leader. The one-minded organization of the patriarchal family is reproduced in a dictatorship, accompanied by the silencing of dissident views, stripping the individual of agency and concentrating all legitimacy and responsibility on the father/leader. In this sense the concepts of *authorization*, a mechanism supporting men in retaining power as a group, and *marginalization*, which prevents women or a certain group of men from obtaining power, explain the institutionalization of hegemonic masculinity through patriarchal authoritarianism. These concepts prove particularly useful in examining the relevance of stories featuring female characters and female sexual desire against the backdrop of a patriarchal system that promotes a normative conceptualization of femininity and attempts to naturalize the female as mothers, sisters and child-bearers while obscuring sexual desire.

In the context of Arab and Muslim societies the relevance of transgressive female sexual behaviour has been famously addressed in the works of Nawal el-Saadawi and Fatima Mernissi, perhaps the founders of contemporary Arab feminist thinking in their reflections on the patriarchal perspectives towards the role of women and female sexuality. In their pivotal works el-Saadawi and Mernissi pioneered a scientific approach to female sexuality in Arab and Muslim societies which stresses the subtle relationship between the repression or the concealment of the female's sexual drives and the preservation of an order that gives centrality to the male.[32] Mernissi's analysis of female sexuality as *fitna*, or a source of disorder, demonstrates how women openly expressing their libido are framed as a considerable challenge to the institution of patriarchy, with deep religious and political implications, concluding that women's sexual instincts are fundamentally understood as a threat to the worldly order. Although the significance of the term *fitna*, embodied by women, encompasses various positive and negative connotations, in the context of the relationship between men and women, it ultimately represents a vital threat to the male's stability and well-being.[33] In addition to el-Saadawi and Mernissi's studies, other studies with a focus on the traditional models of masculinity and femininity in the Middle East have substantiated this approach, and have established how the construction of gender roles is closely linked to notions of honour and shame. In this traditional conceptualization of femininity, chastity and purity are the defining traits of the ideal model of woman.[34] Connecting the relevance of these views to neopatriarchy with studies looking at the relationship between gender-motivated fiction and political change in parallel with the historical events in Syria allows us to grasp the political implications of Tamir's textual corpus in the context of literary and ideological developments.

These approaches to literature, history, gender and ideology are brought together into an analytical framework which looks chronologically at the developments in the representations of male and female characters. However, this outlook by no means regards literature as a mere reflection of ideology but rather explores literature as existing within ideology and outside of it: how literature distances itself from a certain worldview while illuminating the reader about the effects of that worldview on the lived experiences of men and women.[35] Analysing Tamir's works and the historical conditions that have produced them, this study looks at the relationship between the forces of patriarchy and authoritarianism and the lived experiences of individuals represented by the stories' protagonists; it explores gender roles as performed by Tamir's protagonists as both the reflection and transgression of norms and hierarchies; it investigates how the stylistic and formal strategies employed by this writer signal his affiliation to a predominant worldview and a form of subversion to it.

Looking at Lebanese fiction writing from the post-war period, Samira Aghacy argues for the increasingly significant transformations in the realm of gender roles. In particular, her study explores the new forms of male identities engendered by the trauma of war, exploring them as changing in accordance with the social, economic and political events in the region.[36] With regards to Syrian literature and to Tamir's works specifically, a similar approach can be pursued to assess the new configurations of masculinity that his works project in the context of the broader, albeit bloodless, political trauma represented by the collapse of consensus and of all notions of ideological and political unity. The gendered dimension that this process of collapse and defeat possesses entails a diminished degree of agency for the male as the primary actor in the political arena. The quest for emancipation and modernization, exemplified by the optimism of stories like 'Rabīʿ fī al-ramād', which appeared for the first time in 1960, as well as other stories characterized by uncertainty, disenfranchisement and marginalization, was typified by the central role of male characters and by the accessory presence of women. The failure of the project from which those stories derived their vitality and inspiration and the persistence of authoritarian and arbitrary rule, similar to the shock of the Lebanese civil war, have produced new gender identities in an author like Tamir, often associated with a sense of anxiety and uncertainty. The nature and the significance of such transformations are analysed and considered giving relevance to the recurrence of roles, traits and characteristics attached to male and female protagonists.

Analysing Tamir's disenfranchised protagonists as victims of society, patriarchy and authoritarianism, Emma Westney proposes a broad categorization dividing characters into two main groups: those wielding power and those stripped of power, further dividing the latter into three subgroups: the café man, the historical hero, and the child.[37] Interestingly enough, female characters do not feature on this list, and the focus rests exclusively on men as represented in positions of subordination in relation to the subgroup of power-wielding characters represented by fathers, policemen, judges, teachers, kings and men of religion. The following chapters scrutinize different configurations of masculinity and femininity in relation to patriarchy and the authoritarian state to demonstrate the political relevance of the gendered dimension of Tamir's stories. In particular, the aim is to both validate the anti-authoritarian stance his stories put forward and deconstruct their language to determine their conformity or subversion to a patriarchal worldview. In its effort to determine the political potential of Tamir's representations of male and female protagonists, and how they channel subversion of or compliance to a patriarchal worldview, this study is motivated by the desire to clarify the variety of transformations that his works have undergone in relation to the changes in the relationship between cultural production, ideology and authoritarianism. By looking at patriarchy and dynamic configurations of masculinity and femininity as represented in Tamir's stories, this study also challenges the binary opposition between state censors and supposedly dissident authors bringing into view the capacity fiction possesses to redress the balance and challenge or reinforce an authoritarian vision, especially one that attempts to naturalize systems of signification. For this purpose, literature reproduces, interiorizes and ultimately transforms the univocality imposed by the discourse of authoritarianism into a multifarious view on the human condition.

1

From commitment to exile

Zakariyya Tamir, the forefather of the modern Syrian short story

This chapter introduces Zakariyya Tamir's life and career, as well as the main stylistic and thematic elements of originality of his works. Tracing his beginnings as a writer back to the late 1950s, this part brings into the discussion of this writer's trajectory aspects such as the crucial role that literary magazines played in the publication and distribution of short stories in the 1950s and 1960s. Magazines such as *Al-Ādāb* and *Shiʿr* played a key role in promoting committed, modern, nationalist and progressive authors to the general public, as well as the centrality of existentialism and socialist realism in the literary debates in which Tamir took part.

This chapter looks at his very early stories in comparison with the literary trends popular in Syria and elsewhere in the Middle East and examines the formal peculiarities of Tamir's works and of the avant-garde aesthetics his stories contributed to introduce in the Arabic short story at the time of his beginnings as a writer. Situating Tamir's trajectory in the context of different conceptualizations of literary commitment popular in Syria and the Arab East in the decades between the 1950s and late 1970s, the first part of the chapter explores the peculiarly autonomous idea of commitment to which the author subscribed to as being intimately linked with a complex engagement with aesthetics. In particular, it interrogates the significance of political affiliation and commitment amongst Arab writers after the pivotal events of 1967 and 1978, as well as Tamir's position with regards to the Syrian uprising from his self-imposed exile in England.

The literary debate in Syria and the Arab East 1948–78

Tamir was born in the al-Baḥṣa neighbourhood of Damascus on 2 January 1931. Recounting his upbringing in an interview, Tamir described the environment he grew up in as 'proud of its ignorance' because no one in his household read.[1] In 1944, at the age of thirteen he was forced to leave school to provide for his family by working as a blacksmith first and later in a variety of other manual professions. Despite being a personality deeply rooted in his native city, who rarely left Syria and had little knowledge of foreign languages, since a young age Tamir was exposed to both Arabic and European literature in translation. An indication of his early exposure to European authors can be found in one of his very first stories, 'Qaranfula lil-asfalt al-mut'ab' (A carnation for the tired tar), in which one of the protagonists mentions, 'We're all crazy. Dostoevsky is a fool, Sartre is an idiot who doesn't love the sun, Rimbaud is a rude child, Tchaikovsky is a sad frog, Lorca is a dark nightingale, Kafka is a cockroach and James Mason is a drum'.[2] Tamir's first short stories were published in the late 1950s in Syrian and Lebanese literary magazines such as *al-Nuqqād*, *al-Ādāb*, and *al-Thaqāfa*. In this early stage of his career, it was only thanks to the moral support provided by Sāmī al-Jundī, at the time the United Arab Republic's Minister of Information and Propaganda,[3] that Tamir pursued his ambitions as a short-story writer.[4] Later, the Palestinian poet, critic and translator Salma Khaḍrā' al-Jayyūsī encouraged him to collect the stories that he had previously published in local magazines into a book. Khaḍrā' al-Jayyūsī in turn proposed his stories to Syrian poet Yūsuf al-Khāl, editor of the Beirut-based magazine *Shi'r*, who decided to publish his first collection *Ṣahīl al-jawād al-abyaḍ* immediately afterwards. In 1961, the first public recognition for his work came from *al-Ādāb*, which awarded his story 'Thalj ākhir al-layl' (Snow late at night), later included in his second collection, the prize for the best story.

In the years between 1957 – when the first story by Tamir appeared in *al-Nuqqād* – and the late 1970s, heated debates on the role of literature and intellectuals characterized the field of cultural production in Syria and in the broader Arab East. The defeat of the Arab armies in 1948, resulting in the loss of Palestine, and Arab nationalist enthusiasm had contributed to the spread of a conceptualization of cultural creativity that considered literature as organic to the struggle for the emancipation of the Arab nation.[5] The establishment of the State of Israel in particular, and the expulsion of hundreds of thousands of Palestinians from their land affected the entire region more directly on a political level. The trends in cultural production too represented to a large extent a reflection of this event, still referred to, to this day, as the *nakba* 'the catastrophe'. As Edward Said noted in his analysis of formal transformations that the Arabic novelistic tradition underwent in the years following 1948, those events exerted an unprecedented degree of pressure on cultural production and its impact cannot be underestimated, as they 'put forward a monumental enigma, an existential mutation for which Arab history was unprepared'.[6]

The issue of Palestine represented one amongst other major aspects which shaped the direction of the cultural establishment. Literary criticism, freedom of expression, the relationship with the West, the role of the Arab cultural heritage (*al-turāth*), the role of Islam and religion in general were but a few of many controversial questions that stirred the debates taking place largely in local literary magazines such as the Lebanese *al-Ādāb*. The influence of social realism on literary commitment in the 1950s and 1960s, and the social and historical developments that motivated this trend are exemplified by the experience of this Lebanese monthly periodical,[7] established by the novelist Suhayl Idrīs in 1953, which promoted 'committed literature' (*al-adab al-multazim*). *Al-Ādāb* – as Idrīs explained in the editorial note to the first issue – fulfilled a widespread need amongst young Arab intellectuals for a periodical dedicated to the mutually influential relationship that literature entertains with society.[8] *Al-Ādāb*'s trajectory in the decades since its establishment until the 1980s epitomizes the variety of concerns that contributed to shape the literary field in those years. Arab nationalism, in a variety of interpretations (humanist, socialist, revolutionary), functioned as the overarching ideology that motivated the efforts of many Arab literary magazines, as well as organizations like the Syrian Writers' Collective.[9] The latter was established in Damascus in 1951 by a group of eight Syrian writers with an overtly socialist realist agenda and motivated by the desire to encourage works by Syrian writers, whose numbers were at that time smaller than their Lebanese and Egyptian counterparts.[10] Both *al-Ādāb* and the Syrian Writers' Collective represented prominent cultural institutions in Syria and the Arab East between the 1950s and 1970s, landmarks that assist us in situating Tamir's early oeuvre. On the one hand, *al-Ādāb* served as a fundamental platform for essays, short stories and novel excerpts, and Tamir published many of his early short stories in the pages of this magazine between 1958 and 1962. On the other hand, the Syrian Writers' Collective adopted an understanding of commitment similar to *al-Ādāb*'s in fostering a generally committed notion of literature, but gradually transitioned to play a fundamental role in spreading a peculiarly Marxist notion of commitment.[11]

The 1950s were a period of intense political upheaval in Syria and across the Arab Mashriq. Syria alone witnessed six coups and joined Egypt, now led by Jamāl 'Abd al-Nāṣir's Free Officers, in the United Arab Republic from 1958 to 1962.[12] The political orientation Tamir assumed in this period as a young writer, and whether or not he joined the Syrian Communist Party, remains a subject for discussion. In his introduction to his analysis of Tamir's stories 'Abd al-Razzāq 'Īd claims that the state of disenfranchisement and poverty he had experienced, and the desire to associate himself with the local writers and intellectuals, pushed Tamir to join the party – which according to 'Īd played a fundamental role in the establishment of the Syrian Writers' Collective – but he was expelled in 1956.[13] With regard to his affiliations, in an article published many years later in al-Taḍāmun,[14] and revived in 2016 on his Facebook personal page,[15] Tamir recounts his affiliation to the Arab Writers' Association (*Jam'iyyat al-Udabā' al-'Arab*). According to Tamir, the association was established in 1958 for the specific purpose of counteracting the activities of the Syrian Writers' Collective, the latter described by Tamir as inspired by the ideals of Khālid Bakdāsh (leader of the Syrian Communist Party from 1930 until his death in 1994[16]) and Andrei Zhdanov (Stalin's emissary of cultural affairs). In turn, Tamir describes the Arab Writers' Association as 'a group of stray wandering writers who despised any form of literary or social constraint, who had dreams to change the world and to change literature to elevate humanity, to encourage free creativity and to destroy old prisons erected in the name of refined writing'.[17] The Arab Writers' Association, however, was to remain a short-lived experience, and the Syrian authorities closed it down following the establishment of the United Arab Republic in 1958.

Following his first publications and success, Tamir took up a position in the Translation and Publication Department of the Syrian Ministry of Culture (1960–3), and in 1963 he published his second collection *Rabī' fī al-ramād* through the Ministry's publishing house. In 1969, he participated actively in the establishment of the Arab Writers' Union in Syria and occupied the position of deputy chairman of the organization between 1973 and 1975. His third collection of short stories, *al-Ra'd*, came out in 1970 followed by *Dimashq al-ḥarā'iq* in 1973. Both collections feature short stories that had appeared at different times in *al-Ādāb*, in *al-Ma'rifa*, the Syrian Ministry of Culture's literary magazine of which he was editor-in-chief from 1978 to 1980, as well as in *al-Mawqif al-Adabī* the Arab Writers' Union's official organ of which he was the editor-in-chief from 1972 to 1975.

When Tamir appeared on the literary scene, Egyptian and Lebanese short-story writers had represented the most significant examples of stylistic maturation of the genre and its ramification into different sensibilities, mostly realist and romantic. In Syria, short-story writers such as Sa'īd al-Ḥūrāniyya, Fu'ād al-Shāyb, and 'Abd al-Salām al-'Ujaylī – in turn strongly influenced by a generation of writers from the 1940s and of the 1950s, namely Yaḥyā Ḥaqqī and Yūsuf Idrīs from Egypt and Tawfīq Yūsuf 'Awwād from Lebanon – had paved the way for the modernist sensibility that emerged in the 1960s, embodied by the more complex and sophisticated literary style of authors like Tamir.[18] The impact of pioneering works of local Syrian contemporary literature on Tamir is undeniable. Their style and most importantly their anti-colonialist and socialist political ideas inspired Tamir in a way that reading their works pushed him to compose his own stories, something the author himself acknowledged, justifying his literary endeavours with a desire to enrich the range of stylistic features and themes that the genre had hitherto addressed.[19] Through the introduction of new techniques and themes Tamir's works in this period innovated the Arabic short story in terms of both style and content, consolidating the modern sensibility and surpassing the sentimental and realist forms.[20] The brief, photographic style of writing that was to become his trademark, as well as the remarkable presence of forlorn, disenfranchised characters represent two major elements of innovation that the stories of this period introduced through the stream of consciousness and the exploration of the inner self. This mirrored a changing social and political reality moving gradually towards a sense of uncertainty, questioning and examination.[21] Stylistically, the feeling is captured through snapshots characterized by brevity and by the point of view of characters that – in Frank O'Connor's definition of the modern short-story's archetype – represented those 'submerged population groups'. Unlike the novel and its protagonists' capacity to engender the readers' affinity, O'Connor highlights the short story's tendency to be populated by non-heroic and estranged characters at the margins of society.[22] For the Arabic short story this introspection and retreat into the inner space of the protagonists represented an important development, a significant transformation because it affected the political dimension of the text and made Tamir's style stand out in Syria and elsewhere in the Arab-speaking world.[23] Stylistically, a further element of originality in this period is represented by the extensive use of fantasy and dream, in which the boundaries between life and death, past and present, reality and imagination are often blurred and confounded.

The individualist orientation in Tamir's style is the most remarkable trait of his writing in this period. Many of his early stories possess an autobiographical tone, as well as aspects of similarity with the works of French existentialists – which had been introduced and made popular in the Arab world by literary magazines. The rise of existentialism in the Arab world served as the foundation for the transition from realism to modernism, and the impact of authors such as Albert Camus shaped a modern literary sensibility.[24] The influence of the French existentialists on Arab litterateurs in this period was undoubtedly remarkable,[25] their influence being manifest also in the inspiration that Sartre's magazine, *Les Temps Modernes*, provided to *al-Ādāb*'s founder Suhayl Idrīs.[26] Like Sartre, *al-Ādāb*'s founder saw writers as part of a project in which freedom is the fundamental principle to generate change, a project that envisaged action and morals as deeply entwined.[27]

Tamir and the debate on commitment and socialist realism

Tamir's protagonists' individualism, the symbolism of his stories and the affinity to French existentialism contradicted in a variety of ways the principles of socialist realism that had become prominent in Syria in the 1950s through the efforts of the Syrian Writers' Collective. Socialist realism in Syria advocated a specific conceptualization of literary commitment, rejecting contemporary literary and philosophical tendencies such as existentialism, Freudianism and symbolism on the basis of their European origins, and because of their incompatibility with Arab nationalism and class struggle. In addition, the cultural debate was influenced significantly by Russian socialist realism.[28] This approach to literature, in the way it was articulated in Russia in the 1930s, and adopted by founders of the Syrian Writers' Collective, associated aesthetic strategies that did not serve the social function to a bourgeois or imperialist point of view. Refusing to respond to the demands of socialist realism, according to which fiction must deliver a powerful message on society and class struggle, the cruel reality of exploitation, hardship and disenfranchisement against which Tamir's forlorn protagonists grapple is countered instead by an alternative universe of dream and imagination.

Building on O'Connor's conceptualization of the short story and his analysis of the genre's ideology, Sabry Hafez has also stressed the disparity between the short story and the novel in Marxist terms highlighting the former's inclination to explore human loneliness, incomprehension, ridicule and injustice. While the novel seeks to create a sense of community and belonging around protagonists that the reader can identify with, the short story takes the reader into the unexplored quarters of that community and deals with those individuals which the novel's larger portrayal overlooks.[29] It does not come as a surprise then that the champions of socialist realism in Syria between the 1950s and 1970s devoted their outpourings of accolades to a novelist like Ḥannā Mīna (b. 1924), while criticizing Tamir's short stories. While both were members of a new generation of writers hailing from urban working-class backgrounds that emerged in the 1950s, Mīna always considered himself a socialist realist,[30] and his novels enjoyed the praises of the socialist realist critics for their capacity to represent the vicissitude of the Syrian people under the French mandate[31] with a focus on the hardships endured by the proletariat. In his introduction to Mīna's 1954 novel *al-Maṣābīḥ al-zurq* (Blue Lights),[32] Shawqī Baghdādī – a founding member of the Syrian Writers' Collective – celebrates this novel for its capacity to narrate life in Syria through the portraying of ordinary people's lives during the Second World War. Baghdādī's view is echoed in Aḥmad Muḥammad al-ʿAṭiyya's *al-Iltizām wa al-thawra fī al-adab al-ʿarabī al-ḥadīth* (Commitment and revolution in modern Arabic literature)[33] and Muḥammad Kāmil al-Khaṭīb's *ʿĀlam Ḥannā Mīna al-riwāʾī* (Ḥannā Mīna's novelistic world),[34] which extol Mīna's realistic depiction of the nation from a working-class point of view. On the other hand, Tamir has never tried his hand at the novel, but being a member of the working class born to a modest background, his very first stories in particular possess strong autobiographical connotations and are sometimes told in the first person by a nameless narrator. The main difference with Mīna's style, however, does not reside only in the degree of realism in his portrayals of working-class experience of disenfranchisement and alienation – which features prominently, especially in Tamir's first collection – but more fundamentally in the genre's predisposition to singularity and marginality to the detriment of the collective experience.

The relevance of Tamir's literary output and the controversy that these elements of novelty stirred at the time is manifest in the prominence afforded to his writing by two texts that appeared in Syria between 1974 and 1977: *al-Adab wa-al-idıyūlūjiyā fī Sūriyya 1967–1973* (Literature and ideology in Syria 1967–1973)[35] by Nabīl Sulaymān and Bū 'Alī Yāsīn contains an entire section on this writer,[36] providing a detailed critique of his third collection, *al-Ra'd*; and *Ma'ārik thaqāfiyya fī Sūriyya 1975–1977* (Cultural battles in Syria 1975–1977), whose second part is entirely devoted to a series of contributions on Tamir's work by Syrian literary critics.[37] In an essay in the latter collection, 'About the world of Zakariyyā Tamir's'[38] by the young writer and critic Muḥammad Kāmil al-Khaṭīb, Tamir's literary style and themes are criticized for their lack of commitment and their 'nihilist retreat' visible in self-focused protagonists who are 'not interested in social battles, attempt to withdraw from the battlefield, and dream of perpetual sleep and death'.[39] In the eternal and universal conflict between the two abstract concepts of individual and society – al-Khaṭīb argues – Tamir's characters choose to withdraw from the battlefield and isolate themselves in a world of dream and imagination. By dissecting and criticizing the ideological shortcomings of each individual collection published by Tamir between 1960 and 1973, condemning his writing for failing to impact and foster change, al-Khaṭīb's article exemplifies the cultural atmosphere in which Tamir's first writings appeared. For al-Khaṭīb, Tamir's divorce from Marxist and nationalist commitment becomes manifest particularly in the removal of the episode (*ḥāditha*), as well as in characters who dream of perpetual sleep and death refusing to engage in social battles. And even in stories in which the protagonist loses prominence to the advantage of the plot and the overarching theme addressed – a transformation al-Khaṭīb detects first in Tamir's *Rabī' fī al-ramād* – no empowerment is achieved, and the characters remain largely helpless in the face of a harsh environment.[40]

Compared to its predecessor (*Ṣahīl al-jawād al-abyaḍ*, whose stories are usually told by the narrator in the first person) *Rabi' fī al-Ramād* represents for al-Khaṭīb a major turning point with regards to the main theme in Tamir's short stories: the conflict between the individual and society. However, although in this collection modern tools and systems of torture and killing do appear, there is not a significant change in the nature of Tamir's protagonists, whom al-Khaṭīb considers largely 'negative' (*silbīyya*) for their refusal to take part in the on-going battle against authoritarianism. In *al-Ra'd*, according to al-Khaṭīb, the conflict between specific actors in society begins to crystallize with its most recurrent protagonists, a trademark of Tamir's later stories: policemen and helpless civilians. In this collection, the policeman acquires epic and pseudo-philosophical traits, representing forces that oppress the individual. In this context, the police officer can be interpreted as a symbol for the outside world of society at large as perpetually opposed to the individual. 'But who is this policeman?' – asks al-Khaṭīb – 'Is he just a policeman? Or is he a metaphor for the ruling authoritarian regime? Or is he perhaps a metaphor for those forces eternally opposed to the individual?'[41] To exemplify what he considers the author's nihilism and uncommitted style, al-Khaṭīb proposes an interpretation of an excerpt from Tamir's 'Alladhī aḥraqa al-sufun' (The one who burnt the ships).

> The first day hunger was created.
> The second day music was created.
> The third day books and cats were created.
> The fourth day cigarettes were created.
> The fifth day coffee shops were created.
> The sixth day anger was created.
> The seventh day birds were created
> and their nests hiding on trees.
>
> And on the eighth day interrogators were created, and they descended upon the cities accompanied by policemen, prisons and steel chains. [42]

Tamir's own special reinventing of the Book of Genesis, according to al-Khaṭīb, exemplifies the author's abstract view of the oppressive force of the state as detached from the historical conditions that produced it.[43] While he acknowledges that the stories do possess a specific political significance, al-Khaṭīb's criticism takes this story as a crucial example that illustrates the author's universalization of oppression embodied by the policemen, removing it from the specific context of contemporary authoritarianism. 'Because'

– al-Khaṭīb continues – 'although Tamir's stories denounce oppression and abuses, they are also, somehow, saying that oppression and abuse are eternal. In this way, the author escapes the clutches of a bitter reality, and embarks on a more bitter journey through which he aims to destroy life in its entirety'.[44]

Socialist realism's idea of the literary output as a message bearer with a clear role in the struggle against the dominance of the petty bourgeoisie, and its view of the author as 'the artist in uniform'[45] was met from a very early stage with Tamir's unreserved opposition. In particular, in his 1972 interview with the Syrian Ministry of Culture's literary journal *al-Ma'rifa*, as well as in an article published in the *al-Ba'th* newspaper, part of the heated debate stirred by al-Khaṭīb's observations, Tamir started clarifying a position on commitment in literature that was closer to Sartre's. Himself a champion of politically motivated literature, Sartre called for a high degree of autonomy of the artist by making a distinction between *committed* and *tendentious* art: the former being concerned with fundamental attitudes, rendering the author's stance ambiguous to the eyes of socialist realists; the latter, intended to generate specific transformations in society, displaying a more overtly partisan style.[46] In the Arab world a similar approach to literary commitment – which albeit animatedly debated was hardly ever put into question – was first promoted by the Egyptian Ṭāhā Ḥusayn, who illustrated his understanding of the writer's engagement in the pages of *al-Ādāb*.[47] After all, Ḥusayn is considered to have been the first Arab intellectual to translate Sartre's ideas into Arabic, and the first to have introduced the concept of commitment (*iltizām*) into the literary debate,[48] although advocating for the freedom of the artist from the chains of ideological obligation.[49] In Tamir's response to al-Khaṭīb's observations, there is a noticeable hardening of the debate, but also more relevantly a manifest disparity in the conceptualization of literature and the aesthetic autonomy that Tamir claimed as a writer, a notion affiliated more closely with the general trends proposed by Sartre, as well as by *al-Ādāb* and Ḥusayn.

> Literature in our nation is indeed a poor devil, and if it could take the shape of a human being in the flesh, it would choose that of a beggar sitting by the door of mosques and churches with his head down, wearing shabby clothes. Writers who are devoted to their environment and to a form of literature distant from the spasmodic and loud zeal are indeed the orphans at the reconciliation table.

> One of the reasons for this despicable situation is the emergence of a clique of critics and litterateurs (*udabāʾ*) that claims to be the only honourable and fully aware group, the only repository of scientific and objective thought, which in the name of the present situation and its problems disregards all new literary output with harsh categorisations and judgements that remind me of a butcher that prefers to drink blood over vodka. This groups snipes its unappealable sentences indiscriminately at writers that it considers reactionaries, because they don't criticise colonialism, or traitors of the working class, because they talk about music, and cats and flowers (as if music, cats and flowers were members of the central intelligence), as well as at writers that this group considers shut off from reality because they don't touch on *fedayyen* (fidāʾīn) patriotism.
>
> This group is constituted by people with different interests and trajectories. Some of them have no literary background, they are more into economics. When they propose their ideas, they rely on the constitution that guarantees freedom of speech. Others are writers who've written extensively using a variety of pens but have produced nothing but drug information slips. Others were writers in the past, then they fell asleep for ages, and suddenly woke up and came out of their graves, expressing their loathing of anything written during their hibernation. The only thing uniting these people is their superficial view on literature and its role. Literature in their opinion is designated to liberate Palestine, Arabstan[50] and al-Andalus; for them it is up to literature to combat illiteracy and spread awareness amongst the citizens, and it is responsible for the persecution of South Africa's black population.[51]

The same concerns with the rigid tenets of socialist realism and its widespread influence amongst Syrian literary critics underpinned Tamir's interview with *al-Maʿrifa*, in August 1972, in which he laments a lack of interest from Syrian literary critics in the formal aspects of literature.[52] The entire interview revolves around the state of literary criticism in Syria and in the Arab world. The text's political message and its affiliation with specific ideological trends is, according to Tamir, all that Syrian critics focused their efforts on, thereby reducing the text to a mere didactic container of ideological approaches and instructions on how to address this or that issue afflicting Syrian and Arab societies.[53] While Tamir maintains that commitment to the causes of his or her own society should be a must for every writer aspiring to exert any degree of impact on their environment, he, however, laments that literary criticism in the Arabic-speaking world requires writers to deliver 'national liberation, education of the masses, to build factories, dams, hospitals and parks'.[54] The interview also illustrates Tamir's attention to the autonomy of structure and form, signalling his role in the self-conscious search for styles and techniques that suit content and meaning, a quest that was characteristic of a mature modern sensibility which his works contributed to achieve.[55] In what seems like a tailored interview designed specifically to allow him to counter the attitude of Syrian socialist realist critics – examples of a style of 'vulgar Marxist' literary criticism[56] – Tamir denounces not only their lack of focus on form but especially the excessive emphasis devoted to interpret the political attitude of authors, heedless of the fact that 'we are deceiving ourselves if we believe that a literary work written and published in a country where seventy percent of the population is illiterate, can change the political and social life of the country. It is up to political organizations and not to romantic literature to change the present situation'.[57]

Sulaymān and Yāsīn's *Literature and ideology in Syria 1967–1973* also exhibits an exhortative approach to literary production similar to al-Khaṭīb's, as well as a rigidly ideological and prescriptive approach in their critique of Tamir's stories. This study appeared in 1974 with the explicit intent of addressing the political stagnation which had affected the country since the 1967 setback, to scrutinize its multiple reverberations in literary production between 1967 and 1973. The authors aspired to identify those works that had addressed the struggles of the working class, and the issue of national liberation in Syria and in the wider Arab world.[58] In the essay 'al-ra'd alladhī la yumṭir[u] – majmū'at qiṣaṣ' (The thunder that does not bring rain – a collection of short stories)[59] the authors respond to Tamir's harsh denunciation of the state of literary criticism in Syria, and proceed to dissect the stories of *al-Ra'd* individually, exposing the ideological shortcomings and the petty bourgeois point of view of the author as the collection's main flaws. The strictly Marxist yardstick with which the authors examined this work makes them condemn the author's retreat into the world of dreams, fantasia and individual isolation as a betrayal of his class origins, and his short stories as uncommitted stories that signal the author's abandonment of realism in favour of 'anarchy'.[60] They condemn Tamir's bitter view of society as nihilist, his suggestive style and his disregard for the boundaries of time and space, life and death representing for them the perfect literary device to put forward a pessimistic message.

> He doesn't have the tiniest piece of regard for the necessities of an underdeveloped country going through a transitory phase where the state centralises power leading sometimes to dreadful consequences. He attacks, rejects, destroys, yells, as if that was his way of achieving pleasure. [61]

The criticism Tamir was subjected to at home confirms the independent outlook and unconventional approach to nationalist and revolutionary engagement put forward in his works. At the same time, however, al-Khaṭīb's, Sulaymān's and Yāsīn's essays cannot be considered representative of an entire field of authors and critics. Their essays stirred an animated discussion between a number of other actors in the Syrian literary scene who exposed their approach as superficial and excessively ideological, ultimately failing to recognize the innovations that Tamir's style had brought about.[62] These diverging reactions hint at the decline of a genre – socialist realism – that had hitherto exerted considerable influence on both fiction and literary criticism, shaping the field of cultural production through institutions, publications and events. Such contributions demonstrate the strong influence of Soviet socialist realism on commitment and prose fiction in Syria, and how Tamir's originality fundamentally broke with the dominant ideologically motivated literature, a trend already in decline at the time his first collection was published.

After *ḥadātha*: Fragmentation and the abandoning of totalizing ideology

By the mid-1970s the popularity of the unifying ideologies which had put forward a totalizing, uniform vision of society that emulated European models, began to decline in parallel with the historical events in the area engendering a process of ideological fragmentation.[63] Not only the defeats in the 1967 and 1973 wars against Israel, but also a series of broader transformations altered the inclinations of cultural production from Syria and the wider Arabic-speaking world irreversibly: the attitude towards Israel, the conflict within the Palestinian resistance movement and between the Palestinian resistance movement and Arab regimes, rising inequality and class conflict, the rivalry between the cities and countries historically considered 'central' (Egypt and the Ottoman Bilād al-Shām) and the peripheries (the Gulf and North Africa), the civil war in Lebanon, the rise of Gulf monarchies and of political Islam as a major force in the political arena.[64]

Arabic literature in this period evolved as a consequence of modernism's destructive charge and at the same time as a call to question its values and aspirations, typified by doubt, anxiety and self-critique, replacing the confidence of the previous period. By the early 1970s the form of Tamir's writings – akin to poems and novels published in the same period[65] – displayed the signs of fragmentation in collections containing a large number of stories divided into a series of sub-stories and sub-paragraphs, sometimes bearing different titles, addressing a variety of subjects and plots, embodied by various protagonists with no apparent unity of time and space. This aspect emerges first in *al-Ra'd*, where the same stories that Sulaymān and Yāsīn dissected so meticulously looking for the author's class point of view displayed the signs of stylistic transformations that possess crucial political connotations, perhaps the sign of a postmodern spirit beginning to exert its influence on Arabic writing.[66] The degree to which Tamir's works can be considered postmodern, particularly in the context of postmodernity in contemporary Arabic cultural production, will be discussed in more detail in the last two chapters; however, their political relevance makes them stand out in the stories of this period against the backdrop of the cultural battles raging in Syria at the time of their publication. The Book of Genesis passage quoted earlier, together with numerous other stories from that same period, shows elements of fragmentation of the text, intertextuality and a multiplicity of voices. The fragmented nature of the text signals the author's distancing from the idealist forms of writing advocated by the champions of socialist realism, but is nonetheless charged with strong political connotations, as it draws figures and symbols from the Arabic tradition to address the stringent issues of rising authoritarian coercion.

This becomes particularly manifest in *al-Numūr fī al-yawm al-'āshir*, a compilation of stories central to the developments and transformations in this author's oeuvre because of the formal changes it introduced as well as because of its overtly political tone. The stories of this collection have become classics, have enjoyed the largest number of translations,[67] and have found their place in the Syrian literary tradition for their suggestive depictions of authoritarian practices. The title story of this collection, which can easily be considered Tamir's masterstroke, the one story all readers automatically associate with this writer, does not display any of the aforementioned stylistic transformations, but it is nonetheless relevant in this period for a more manifestly blunt language signalling the urge to address the increasingly invasive nature of the authoritarian state and its ruthless practices of coercion and domination. The story revolves around the eponymous tiger and its forced imprisonment by a nameless tamer, who gradually subdues and domesticates the proverbially untameable animal, starving it and training it to obey the most humiliating commands. Notoriously a proud and invincible animal, the tiger initially refuses to be tamed and chooses to starve rather than obey its new trainer's commands. Pressed by hunger, though, the tiger begins to compromise with its new master in exchange for some meat. Within a few days, the tiger has become submissive and weak and is compelled to convert to vegetarianism in order to survive.

> [. . .] And when the tiger's hunger grew, he tried to eat the hay. He was shocked by the taste and backed away in disgust. But he went back, and gradually became accustomed to it. And on the tenth day, the tamer, his students, the tiger and his cage disappeared, and the tiger became a citizen, and his cage a city.[68]

There are many possible interpretations for this famous story. For example, if we read it as a reaction to the rise of authoritarianism, the tiger metaphorically represents the fate of citizens living under a tyrannical power that dominates, imprisons and starves them until it gradually subdues even the most proud and rebellious. On the other hand, the closure suggests that the process of taming the tiger could be interpreted as a metaphor for the construction of a safe, civilized society – suggested by the closure in which the tiger becomes a 'citizen' – as opposed to the forest where the tiger used to live. Be that as it may, the story is praised for its highly poetical and intense form, as well as for the evocative content, and is usually regarded as Tamir's masterpiece. While authoritarian practices such as arbitrary arrest have been present in Tamir's work since the early 1960s, the stories of the mid- and late 1970s gathered in this collection address despotism and its practices more extensively. It is perhaps this aspect that has earned it its wide popularity in a country dominated to this day by a violent authoritarian regime. The relevance of this story resides also in its allegorical recourse to the world of animals as the literary device to represent authoritarianism and its material as well as intellectual grip on society allegorically, an element present in the Arabic literary tradition since the works of the eighth-century Persian translator Ibn al-Muqaffaʿ.

The end of illusions and exile: The struggle against authoritarianism

> What is this desire for a poor miserable existence, for a false serenity when your life is nothing but toil and hardship? Are you proud of this patience of yours, or do you get a reward for it?
>
> What is this disparity amongst you, when your lord created you equal in body, strength, nature and necessities?
>
> Didn't God create you free, with nothing but light and wind weighing upon you, yet you've insisted on enduring nothing but injustice and oppression? [69]

At this crucial point in Syria's contemporary history, Tamir was at the peak of his popularity after the publication of *al-Numūr fī al-yawm al-ʿāshir* in 1978 and occupied the position of editor-in-chief of *al-Maʿrifa*, the official literary magazine of the Syrian Ministry of Culture and National Guidance. The quote at the start of this section, taken from ʿAbd al-Raḥmān al-Kawākibī's famous *nahda* work *Ṭabāʾiʿ al-istibdād wa maṣāriʿ al-istiʿbād* (The nature of despotism and the struggle against enslavement),[70] was published (under al-Kawākibī's name), by Tamir in his capacity as the journal's editor-in-chief, as the opening editorial of *al-Maʿrifa* in the May 1980 issue. This infuriated the Syrian authorities who, according to Tamir himself, did not realize or pretended not to know al-Kawākibī, despite his towering role in Syria's modern history and indeed the entire Arab world and its nineteenth-century *nahda*. Tamir was dismissed from the position of editor-in-chief for this, copies of *al-Maʿrifa* were confiscated from around Damascus's bookshops.[71] Although it would only seem sensible then to make the connection between the ostracism of Tamir by the Syrian authorities and his decision to leave Damascus a year later, a variety of reasons, including a feeling of disaffection towards the Syrian capital, motivated him to go into self-imposed exile to England.[72]

The advent of the 1980s after all marked the end of an era and the beginning of an entirely new course in the history of Syria and the Arab East, while also inaugurating a new epoch for Arab intellectuals. Historically, the Camp David accords between Egypt and Israel in 1978 marked the end of a thirty-year period of nationalist fervour punctuated by three wars and nearly uninterrupted political upheaval culminating with the outbreak of the Lebanese civil war in 1975. In Syria, widespread episodes of violence between government forces and the

Syrian Muslim Brotherhood in the years between 1976 and 1982 culminated in the Hama massacre of February 1982. For Arab intellectuals, these years marked the beginning of a period characterized by exile and marginality, at the tail end of thirty years of political engagement, coinciding with the loss of autonomy of thought to the overwhelming and invasive presence of military authoritarian regimes.[73] In Syria, surveillance and censorship had been monopolized by the state before the 1980s; however, up to that point intellectuals had managed to carve out spaces for discussion that disappeared with the consolidation of the Assad regime, limiting the choices to courtesanship, imprisonment or exile to Europe.[74] The grip of the one-party state on all forms of dissent – motivated by the mid-1970s turmoil, but in continuity with a trend that had typified Syria's political life since independence – was consolidated, and the figure of President Ḥāfiẓ al-Assad rose prominently to become the 'eternal leader'.[75]

The trends that have influenced Arabic literature in the past four decades (the distancing of writers from ideology, the frequent removal of the novel's setting from the homeland to faraway locations, the combination of a variety of styles and the recourse to intertextual devices that borrow from the Arabic traditional *turāth*) are sometimes associated with an indifferent form of postmodernism. Yet, the disengaged attitude of specifically Western postmodernism and its divorce from any edifying, moral or functional spirit has proven incompatible with the aspirations of contemporary Arab writers, whose concerns by and large remain rooted in the political and social struggles in their countries of origin. The persistence of authoritarianism, the lack of individual and collective rights, the complicity between apparently different, opposing conservative and patriarchal forces of Islamism and authoritarianism, the unresolved Palestinian issue, just to mention a few.[76] These as well as numerous other stylistic and thematic elements remain to this day central to cultural production in the Arab world, even in its postmodern configuration.[77]

In Syria, the literary responses to the longstanding persistence throughout the past four decades of an authoritarian, repressive regime have brought about different approaches to studying the ways in which Syrian writers have articulated their resistance to this situation. A 'new Syrian literature', embodied by new young authors such as Khālid Khalīfa, Samar Yazbak, Rūzā Yāsīn Ḥasan, Manhal al-Sarrāj, 'Abīr Isbir, whose works have appeared in the past two decades has gained unprecedented popularity outside Syria. Whereas the abandonment of grand narratives of nationalism and socialism has become the rule, the concerns of these writers remain fundamentally political.[78] The divorce between ideology and cultural production can be interpreted as part of a wider process of fragmentation that has brought about significant aesthetic transformations, including the emergence of a plurality of voices and styles. Although devoid of the ideological dimension of the previous decades, this style retains a political potential in reasserting the role literature can play in an authoritarian context.[79] The political nature of these novels resides frequently in a taboo-breaking and openly denouncing narration of historical events, such as the 1976–82 turmoil in Khalīfa's *Madīḥ al-Karāhiya* (In Praise of Hatred),[80] or in the equally transgressive representation of the body, female desire and the physical act of love in the works of Yazbek and Ḥasan.[81] The transgressive nature of these novels and their most recurrent themes substantiate the argument of Syrian literature as persistently linked to social, historical and political causes.[82]

Tamir's relocation to the UK was followed by a long period of literary silence and increased journalistic activities. In the 1980s and 1990s, he transitioned from being a literary editor and short-story writer to becoming a full-time commentator in Arabic in the pages of magazines like *al-Nāqid*, *al-Dustūr*, *al-Taḍāmun*, and newspapers such as the London-based *al-Quds al-ʿarabī*.[83] The style of these contributions has remained that of the satirical article, addressing the persistence of authoritarianism in the Arab world. Most of these articles have been compiled into two collections, *Hijāʾ al-qatīl li-qātilihi* (*The victim's satire of his killer*)[84] and *Arḍ al-wayl* (*The Land of Misery*).[85] *Nidāʾ Nūḥ*, the collection that inaugurated the second period of his career, appeared in 1994 for the Lebanese Riyad el-Rayyes Books, followed by *Sa-naḍḥak* (We shall laugh) in 1998, *al-Ḥiṣrim* in 2000 and *Taksīr Rukab* in 2002, also published by Riyad el-Rayyes. He wrote a regular column for the London-based *al-Zamān* newspaper in 2002 and for the Syrian government-controlled *al-Thawra* in 2006.[86] In March 2015 he received the Mahmoud Darwish Award for Freedom and Creativity awarded by the Palestinian Darwish foundation.[87] Earlier awards include the Sultan Bin Ali Al Owais Cultural Foundation's prize for Stories, Novels and Drama in 2001, the Syrian Order of Merit in 2002, the Cairo First Short Story Prize in 2009 and in the same year the Blue Metropolis Literary Prize.

Already in the late 1990s and early 2000s Tamir's stories address the never-changing character of power and politics in Syria not only through allegories but also through a vocabulary that pokes fun at the apparent harmony and stability of the country in a very explicit manner. *Taksīr Rukab* in particular epitomizes the novelty of Tamir's latest works, as it combines ironic and unconventional representations of female sexuality with an explicit and transgressive denouncing of authoritarian practices, perhaps representing a sign of the gradual transformation of Syrian authoritarian culture that Max Weiss has suggested.[88] More than any other in Tamir's oeuvre, this collection needs to be situated in its historical context, to comprehend its singularity and to grasp its implications in the broader field of Syrian cultural production. Published in 2002, it came out ideally at the intersection between the two Syrias, that of Ḥāfiẓ al-Assad and his iron-fist rule and the country his son Bashār inherited. In June 2000, following Ḥāfiẓ al-Assad's death, the Syrian parliament reduced the mandatory minimum age to run as president from forty to thirty-four years, with the explicit intent of allowing Bashār to become the new president. Following the Syrian constitutional procedures, a referendum was held in July 2000 in which Bashār al-Assad won an unrepeated 97 per cent of preferences receiving, at least formally, the official investiture of the Syrian people.[89] Many saluted Bashār al-Assad's election as a new era that could lead Syria to the establishment of a civil society, but the new president soon revealed a political identity in continuity with his father's authoritarian legacy.[90] Various examples from this collection reveal a boldness of language and representations that Syrian fiction was not accustomed to, and that perhaps came as a reaction to the illusory opening of civil society inside Syria in the early 2000s. In one of the stories from *Taksīr Rukab*, the protagonist 'Alī al-Ṭayyib epitomizes the ordinary citizen: he wakes up from a coma after several years only to find out that nothing has changed in his country. His 'baffling illness' not only serves as a pretext to depict a reality of disappointment and frustration but also hints very explicitly at the draining effects of life under an authoritarian, paralysing government whose president 'had not been replaced, nor had he changed. He had become increasingly more healthy and youthful'.[91] The story goes on to enumerate the unchanged list of ministers and the privileges they enjoy from their positions. What has changed, though, are all the enjoyable things 'Alī al-Ṭayyib used to know before his coma. His favourite coffee house, his favourite poet, his favourite actress, a courageous journalist had all disappeared or changed their professions and personas to adapt to the zeitgeist. 'He asked about a river and was told it had dried up. 'Alī al-Ṭayyib then closed his eyes and tried to get back into his coma but his efforts were not successful.'[92] The depiction of the president as looking 'healthier and youthful' is nothing but an ironic depiction of the continuity between the old and deceased father and his young son who took up his legacy. The irony and the dark humour underlying the contrast between a mummified and privileged political establishment on one hand, and the decay of society on the other, successfully bring up two repressed narratives elucidating a reality of abuse: the hereditary nature of power, ironically interpreted by the 'younger' president, and the long murderous record of the Syrian regime and its president who has 'resolved to walk in the funeral processions of all his citizens as well as those of their children and grandchildren.'[93]

The Syrian revolution: Syria speaks

The popular revolution that broke out in March 2011 has changed Syria's future for decades to come. For Syrian artists and purveyors of culture in general it has represented another fundamental watershed, a before-and-after that has left them with a stark choice between indifference or outright support. Numerous Syrian artists belonging to Tamir's generation who still live in Syria have refused to participate in the popular uprising that broke out in March 2011 and have openly voiced their support for the Assad regime, or else remained silent bystanders. Engaged novelists such as Ḥaydar Ḥaydar, Ḥannā Mīna and Nādyā Khūst, once the champions of commitment to socialist realism, as well as actors like Bassām Kūsā and Durayd Laḥḥām, popular in Syria for their anti-regime portrayals in films like Nabīl Māliḥ's *al-Kumbārs* (1993) or in plays such as Muḥammad al-Māghūṭ's *Kāsak yā Waṭan*,[94] have remained in Syria until the present day and have often remained indifferent to the popular movement that seeks to overthrow the Assad regime – often for their own personal safety.[95] This stands in contrast with the new wave of young writers and artists that have emerged since the early 2000s, and have often been forced to leave the country because of their participation in the events of the Syrian revolution with written and filmic recounts of the very first days of demonstrations and sit-ins, as well as with cartoons and short stories published mostly through social media. By way of illustration, the novelists Samar Yazbik and Muṣṭafā Khalīfa, for example, have been at the forefront of a renewed wave of political activism. Yazbik has published two accounts: the first on the early days of the Syrian revolution[96] and the second on her journey through the areas under the control of the armed opposition.[97] Khalīfa's *al-Qawqa'* (The shell)[98] remains one of the most graphic accounts of the horrors of Syria's prisons.[99] The cartoonist 'Alī Farzāt, known for drawing satirical cartoons for years targeting the Syrian regime and security apparatus,[100] was abducted and severely beaten by masked men believed to be regime thugs in August 2011 and has since lived in Kuwait.[101]

For his own part and as a symbolic participation in open support of the Syrian revolution against the regime of Bashār al-Assad, in January 2012 Tamir started a Facebook page, called *al-Mihmāz* (in Arabic 'The Spur'), where he publishes very short stories and brief comments not only satirizing the government with metaphors and allegories but also mentioning its members, the Syrian president and other key figures specifically. He has described this form of social media activism as a necessity, reflecting the urgency of expressing his political position publicly in order to dispel all doubts about his persona and his stance:

> I started believing there was a meticulous execution of a carefully assembled plan that aims at associating certain people with the Syrian Revolution, while side-lining the positions of key Syrian figures in the fields of culture, literature, arts and politics. In short, I found myself deprived of every chance to express my position supporting the Syrian revolution, which I regard as the obvious position, and an extension of my fifty years of writing.[102]

Tamir's enthusiastic, although virtual, participation in the uprising then does not only make his current position clear as an intellectual in the context of the Arab Spring and the Syrian revolution; rather than serving to dispel all doubts about his relationship with the Syrian political establishment, his Facebook activity also represents a peculiar, unforeseen stage of his literary trajectory through which he has channelled the widespread dissident, anti-establishment feelings that the 2011 revolution has revealed. In the same aforementioned interview, one of the very few he has released in his life, the author discusses the events in his country and reveals his controversial opinion about the revolution:

> The Syrian revolution surprised me, but it did not at the same time. This contradiction is due to my belief in the non-existence of a Syrian citizen

> that supports this brutal regime. However, every Syrian citizen has a dual personality, one a covert personality that hates the dominant regime blindly, despises it and wishes its swift demise, and the other personality is overt, publicly supporting the regime, heaping praise on it and obeying all its directives.[103]

The similarity between Tamir's description of the average Syrian citizen's contradictions and Wedeen's analysis of silent compliance to the discourse of the Syrian regime, embodied by the Assad family, is striking. Wedeen's study of Syrian political language and strategies of domination discusses how Syrians deal daily with the demands of the authoritarian regime, displaying loyalty but ultimately acting *as if* they believed the preposterous claims of immortality of the leader, his almighty nature and his steadfast battle against the 'Zionist enemy'.[104] However, while the implications of Tamir's digital experience have not been addressed in detail, it shall suffice to point out the undiminished relevance of political commitment for writers in Syria, exemplified by the controversy stirred by his activism as a necessity to clarify his stance. Unsurprisingly, his overt support for the popular movement has earned Tamir the ostracism of the Syrian regime making it increasingly more difficult for his works to reach Syria's bookshops, particularly his latest effort *Ard al-Wayl* published in 2015 which has remained practically unnoticed inside Syria. On the other hand, a younger generation of artists have welcomed the unexpected decision, and the Creative Memory of the Syrian revolution celebrated his symbolic participation in the revolution with a stamp – part of the Stamps of the Syrian revolution series created by 'Ammār al-Beyk – quoting one of his Facebook posts.[105]

Be that as it may, his open support to the cause of the popular movement against the Assad regime does not cancel out Tamir's history as a prominent modernist, secular member of the Syrian literary and cultural establishment whose career culminated in the awarding of the Syrian Order of Merit in 2002. His acceptance of the award has been interpreted as a sign of loyalty to the Assad regime,[106] signalling a degree of ambiguity in his relationship with both the Syrian regime and its broader ideological camp which further complicates any attempt to categorize his profile employing binary categories even in this polarized post-revolutionary context.[107]

Conclusions

This chapter has shown how the range of themes addressed by most scholars and critics looking at the political significance of Tamir's short stories exclude gender and sexuality from the repository of refrains that typify his works. The focus of most of the secondary literature remains on the textual strategies and the themes Tamir employs to express his anti-authoritarian stance; however, the significance of gender roles as performed by his stories' protagonists as a product and a reaction to authoritarianism has not been addressed. As the following chapters will demonstrate the dissident potential of Tamir's works lies not, or not only in 'the horrified silence'[108] around which his stories revolve. More significantly, the political content of his stories is detectable in the openly realistic or allegorical representations of authoritarian practices, in the denouncing of tyrant and indoctrinating fathers as actors of male-supremacist and familial oppression and atomization that undermine the unifying assumptions of authoritarianism, as well as in the transgressive representations of female sexual desire.

2

Changing masculinity

Ḥadātha, nationalism and authoritarianism in the 1960s and 1970s

As the first chapter has shown, especially in the early period of his career Tamir strived to articulate a form of commitment which achieves the emancipation and freedom of the individual, valuing the aesthetic over the thematic, refusing strict ideological guidelines. Nevertheless, however heated the debate and strenuous in his stance, Tamir's claims for the autonomy of the author and his emancipation from ideological constraints did not signal a divorce from the political aspirations of the various actors in the cultural debates in this period. Regardless of its Marxist, nationalist or peculiarly Sartrean agenda, the overarching project aspired to exert great influence on society, to foster change and modernization, to channel the aspirations for national liberation and class emancipation. When Tamir appeared on the scene, literature by and large drew extensive inspiration from this vision, and his very early short stories of the 1950s and 1960s, although not subscribing to the prescriptive orientation of socialist realism, were an integral part of this project. The sense of unity was exemplified formally by stories structured mostly around one male protagonist, and by a central subject and location.

Drawing on the patriarchal character of nationalism that Ṭarābīshī and Massad[1] have analysed allows us to examine the ways in which Tamir has interpreted the highly polarized standards of behaviour that patriarchy dictates for the male and the female, and the link between patriarchy and authoritarian nationalist discourse. Looking at patriarchy and gender roles in Tamir's oeuvre and in particular at the development of representations of masculinity, this chapter situates these themes in the territory of Arab nationalist discourse in contemporary Syria, as well as in relation to modernism and authoritarianism. The chapter explores the development of male characters to examine the gradual disintegration of a strong model of masculinity and to explore its implications for the representations of both the body and gender roles.[2]

'Rabī̱ʿ fī al-ramād': *Ḥadātha* as destruction of the old order

While Tamir's stories in this period certainly stand out for their focus on individual rather than collective matters, and for their original use of language mixing prose and poetry, stories he originally published in the late 1950s and early 1960s display elements that allow us to situate them in the predominant *ḥadāthī* mood. What Abu Deeb defines as the modernist – or *ḥadāthī* – project for Arab culture and society represented an endeavour to break away from past Arabic and Islamic tradition to transform the future to a secular, emancipatory, nationalist and (frequently) socialist worldview. This project possessed a strong political dimension, common to the entire Arab-speaking world, closely interlinked with the nationalist quest for the liberation of Palestine and resistance to Western colonialism.[3]

The title story of *Rabīʿ fī al-ramād* (Spring in the ashes) epitomizes many of the motifs that are central to the modernist period that Abu Deeb defines as *ḥadāthī*. Underlying the writings of the modernist period is a notion of the past as

> a corpse, a burden, a wasteland which needed blowing up and gutting down; not necessarily in order to destroy it in its entirety, but in order to refashion and reforge it, assimilating the dimensions of creativity to be found in it into a new history, a history which can extend into the future and help shape it as a glorious time of fulfilment.[4]

This is exemplified impeccably by the title of the story which contains significant indications of the concepts that Abu Deeb associates with the *ḥadāthī* cultural project of that period: spring as an allegory for rebirth and ashes as a symbol of a dead past upon which nonetheless the process of revival is built.[5] The story, published originally in *al-Thaqāfa* in 1960, begins by introducing the reader to a nameless city's environment and population, situating the events clearly in modern times (where all people must carry identification documents) and charged with evident Arab-Islamic connotations, pointing clearly in the direction of inequality, religious hypocrisy and patriarchy as its dominant social features. The story revolves around a nameless male protagonist 'who desired avidly to become a flower, a bird or a wondering cloud', who led a spiritless life until he decides to visit a local market and buy himself a woman. The protagonist later introduces himself as Shahriyār to his recently bought spouse, who in turn reveals herself as Shahrazad, the other well-known protagonist of the *One Thousand and One Nights*. As they kiss for the first time and are soon to get intimate, he hears a call to arms, and descends onto the streets to engage in a bloody battle.

As Aghacy points out, a narrative that assigns polarized roles to men and women is typical of nationalism, an ideology embodied by the *fidā'ī* fighter depicted as fully committed to the cause of freedom in contrast to corrupt regimes.[6] The male hero, charged with the values and connotations of the *ḥadāthī* worldview, embodies the stringent necessity for death and destruction in order to achieve change and an 'existence forged by man and free from divine intervention'.[7] Clearly, the protagonist impersonates the positive and courageous *ḥadāthī* hero, who is romantic in his worldview but remains entangled in a struggle against the surrounding environment.

It is only through bloodshed and destruction of the old order embodied by the city that the protagonist eventually accomplishes the final breakthrough necessary for the creation of a new existence founded on love. This process is presented entirely as a male-led enterprise, to which the female remains marginal, an accessory of the male's individual and collective emancipation, and deprived of any sort of agency. Her role remains that of a shallow personality that lets the man take action and perform the fundamental battle while she is first bought at the local market as an object, then implores the man not to leave her when the battle beckons. In the final scene she appears as a different woman, a helpless Eve in a *Tamirian* Garden of Eden: the closure sees the two protagonists walk towards the destroyed city, holding hands affectionately while the sun shines upon them, encapsulating the optimism and hope in a brighter future that the quest for regeneration and modernization involved. The story's structure and setting possess also a further degree of relevance specific to the political context of Syria for the centrality attached to the city as the embodiment of past tradition. While associating the city with the traditional order might seem a contradiction from a modernist point of view, this aspect needs to be situated in the specific context of Syria's social and political milieu in the years following independence. The struggle for power consisted largely in a long confrontation between urban politically conservative forces and the revolutionary drive embodied by what Hanna Batatu in his extensive examination of the country's power struggles in the post-independence period calls 'Syria's peasantry'.[8]

'Raḥīl ilā al-baḥr': *Ḥadātha* as the quest for purification

The elements of originality, rupture and freshness in terms of style and content in Tamir's early stories represent simultaneously a break with and a continuation of the approach followed by the pioneers of modernism in Arabic literature since the mid-twentieth century. These stories display elements that signal the influence of the optimism and fervour that typified Arabic literature in the decades following independence up until the 1960s. In particular, the short stories that Tamir published in the late 1950s and early 1960s maintain a strong modernist and 'committed' stance in their exploration of an individual's hardships in a rapidly changing society going through momentous transformations. National independence, urbanization and inequality, industrialization and alienation, traditional patriarchy and conservative sexual social mores, the growing presence of the state in the lives of individuals, failed political experiments, war and occupation, all form part of the set of concerns that these stories address.

Another story from this period, published originally in *al-Ādāb* in 1960 and included only thirteen years later in *Dimashq al-ḥarā'iq*, 'Raḥīl ila al-baḥr' (Exodus to the sea) is an example of both the modernist themes that dominated the period of the 1950s and 1960s and the rich symbolism that Tamir's stories displayed in this period. The story is one of the longest in Tamir's career (thirty-eight pages), and remains an exception for an author whose style is renowned for its brevity and photographic nature. The story opens with the male protagonist's statement of his wish to travel, symptomatic of his desire for destruction and rebirth, the rejection of the past and the present embodied in his derisive attitude towards religious tradition. The story portrays the adventures the protagonist goes through to attain his freedom, symbolized by the eponymous sea, the source of renovation that Ḥasan strives to reach through an intense series of encounters punctuated by the recurrence of his request to the array of characters he meets to point him in the direction of the sea ('ayna al-baḥr?', where is the sea?). The constant repetition of the word *baḥr* 'sea' – which recurs seventy times throughout the story – highlights the centrality of the concept which guides the protagonists' actions to attain purification from an unjust existence. The distress that typifies the experiences of murder, rape, enslavement and humiliation that the protagonist undergoes and the quest for freedom that these images symbolize reflect the overall mood of a specific period in contemporary Arabic literature motivated by a strong desire for change, and that in Tamir's stories is personified exclusively by male characters.

In another story from the same period, 'al-Jarīma' (The crime) the family joins the authoritarian state against Sulaymān al-Ḥalabī, a name the author borrowed from an historical figure known to have murdered the French general Jean-Baptiste Kleber in Cairo during Napoleon's first *Campaigne d'Egypte*. The victim of an arbitrary arrest at the hands of the local police, the protagonist is taken to the nearest police station because 'on the sixth of June he had a dream in which he killed general Kleber'.[9] Al-Ḥalabī denies the accusations and pleads innocent but is executed after the chief of police summons three unexpected witnesses, al-Ḥalabī's parents and sister, who testify against him and confirm the police's accusations. In this period, more than just a Kafkaesque rebellion against the family as a traditional institution and a desire to escape, the author expresses deep rancour towards parents through stories in which the misery brought about by family members on their children and siblings is connected to the authoritarian state's arbitrariness or contributes to the perpetuation of its oppressive practices.

This uncompromisingly pessimistic depictions of the detrimental, even decapitating, effects of the family's inextricability at the core of human relations, through which Tamir's writing opposes the unquestionability of the patriarchal figure, is a peculiar trait of the early modernist story in his early writings. In the stories of the late 1960s this theme remains central but undergoes important transformations exemplified by a conspicuous corpus of surreal representations that explore dream and fantasia. Later in his career, Tamir employed a markedly more surreal tone that often resorts to hyperbolic representations of the family as an oppressive institution, depicting unlikely encounters and dialogues between the protagonists and their deceased parents, who continue playing an active and usually egoistic role in their children's lives even after their death. The protagonist of 'al-Ṣaqar' (The falcon) from *al-Ra'd* is a prime example of this conflicting relationship, in which parents represent a burden on their children's lives and the family's authority represents the cause of disquiet. As he recites the first surah of the Qur'ān over his deceased father's soul 'pretending to be scared, sad and broken-hearted', the protagonist hears his father shouting at him that he should stop smoking. The protagonist stubs his cigarette immediately but his dead father shouts again, asking him whether he got married.

> Stubbornly I insist and tell him that I don't want to get married and I don't want to be a father, so he starts shouting angrily again and I say to him:
>
> - 'Don't be upset, father, it will harm your health.'
>
> I rush out of the cemetery while my father is still shouting, and I go home where I find my girlfriend lying in bed with her eyes closed. I had asked her to wash my socks but she claims to be tired so I slaughter her with a firm hand.[10]

The compressed unit of time and space in which the events take place puts dramatic emphasis on the connection between the assertive and unquestionable authority of patriarchal figures and the misery the protagonist brings about in his own family. The narrator seems anxious to stress the inextricable cause-effect relationship between the marital misfortune of the protagonist and his background of patriarchal traditions and institutions, which he cannot escape even after his father's demise. A strain of pessimism characterizes these depictions, and the hero seems to have no alternative but to succumb to the almost immortal resilience of patriarchal figures and traditions.

'Al-Qabw' and 'al-Badawī': *Ḥadātha* as the revolt against patriarchy and exploitation

This anti-patriarchal element of the *ḥadāthī* period is intimately linked to the strong autobiographical dimension exemplified more manifestly by stories such as 'al-Qabw' (The basement)[11] published originally in the *al-Thaqāfa* magazine in June 1958 and included later in *Ṣahīl al-jawād al-abyaḍ* in 1960.

The basement referred to in the title, an image that recurs frequently in Tamir's oeuvre as a symbol of poverty and disenfranchisement, is where the nameless protagonist lives with his mother, a place of deprivation and despair that he constantly seeks to escape from through imagination and daydreaming. The autobiographical element becomes manifest in a variety of stories from this period, but perhaps this is the most striking example because, although he remains nameless, the narrator/protagonist informs the reader he was born in 1931 like the author.

> As we sat in a café separated from the street by a glass wall, my friend suggested I avoid reading books. The midday sun that was inundating the street was as beautiful as an attractive female body and I said to him: – 'I was born in 1931. My mother hasn't died yet. The whole world is miserable.'[12]

The original use of poetic language and suggestive images, particularly in the stories involving the description of the female body and of the feelings its view elicits in the protagonist, distinguishes Tamir's writing in this period. The combination of the *ḥadāthī* tone with the evident influences of surrealism and existentialism contribute to the focus on the male protagonists and their affliction, relegating the female as the means to escape a harsh reality. The language usually describes insignificant actions with attention to detail but with little suggestiveness, almost as if they were mindless activities. The contrast between the monotonous tone employed to describe these seemingly mindless actions and the explosion of metaphors and evocative images that overflows the language as soon as women appear, amplifies the differences between the representations of male and female protagonists. After wandering aimlessly through the city, the protagonist returns to the basement to find his mother waiting for him. The entire scenario produces in him an overwhelming sense of despair and a disgust that cause him to throw up and collapse in his own vomit and drift into a dream. The dream scene that follows is particularly relevant for its fashion of representing female characters, not as multidimensional social actors but as bodies to be enjoyed and accessories to the protagonist's alienation. The scene takes place in a hall filled with music, a theme usually associated with the female body, where a woman invites the protagonists to dance. The following excerpt exemplifies the suggestive poetical connotations the language displays in the illustration of the female body and its sexual charge.

> She looked lovelier than a crimson sky. I shivered every time her lips opened, revealing a smile whose seductiveness penetrated me like a fine spray of perfume. A river of hot blood awakened, surging youthfully under vicious white lights. A wild desire to sip the wine of the mad deity harboured in her body overwhelmed me. My mouth touched upon the naked flesh of the shoulder and started slowly savouring a kind of pleasure that gave me heaps of inebriating shudders. Suddenly I was astonished by a disgusting change. The flesh started to decay, crumble and drop in small fragments that smelt awfully. This transformation bewildered me, I stepped back frightened and went towards the door, which I kicked open and got out, a long cold laughter following me.[13]

While men have agency in their struggle against social constraints, or helplessly succumb to injustice and deprivation, female protagonists possess diametrically different characteristics. In stories enacted mostly by male characters, women appear as the protagonist's mother or as young attractive girls possessing an exclusively bodily dimension. The accurate description of their bodies' attractiveness is charged with poetical connotations that contribute to intensify the impact that the appearance of female protagonists on the scene exerts on the male protagonist.

The strong disparity in the representations of male and female characters in the *ḥadāthī* period is epitomized more manifestly by 'al-Badawī'.[14] As pointed out in the introduction, the importance of dating these stories to their original publication cannot be overstated. The character of the protagonist and the denouncing of material and intellectual deprivation are better understood in relation to the period from the late 1950s to the mid-1960s. As is the case with multiple stories from his first five collections 'al-Badawī' too had already been previously published and was only later included in *Dimashq al-ḥarā'iq*, which appeared in 1973. Tamir published this story originally in *al-Ādāb* in October 1962 and the text contains minor modifications in its 1973 version, which, however, do not affect its structure and contents significantly. The only relevant difference is in the female protagonist's name Samīra, which in the 1973 version replaces the original Samīḥa.[15] The thirteen-year time span that separates the story's original publication in *al-Ādāb* from its incorporation in *Dimashq al-ḥarā'iq* compels us to situate this story in Tamir's very early period to which the stories analysed in this section belong. The *ḥadathī* character emerges again prominently in the desire for freedom and emancipation from the constraints imposed by the traditional patriarchal family. Yet, the story also possesses a further element of originality in its existentialist attitude to love and death, as well as in the textual strategies it displays. The story – the longest in Tamir's career, consisting of approximately forty pages – begins with the protagonist Yūsuf (also a recurrent name for the stories' male protagonists) taking part in a funeral march 'because he did not have anything else to do'.[16] Akin to most of Tamir's protagonists in this period, Yūsuf is a male factory worker living in a dark small basement, previously used for firewood storage, the symbol of his disenfranchisement. After attending the funeral of an unknown woman called Layla, he returns home to his basement, and again the narrative technique proceeds almost mindlessly in its description of everyday actions and gloomy thoughts, which prepares for the female protagonist's entrance.

> He inserted the copper key into the lock and turned it, he opened the door and went in, closing the door behind him. In that moment, he was overcome by the feeling that he was distant from the world, estranged from the white roaring day coursing through the streets.
>
> . . .
>
> he stretched on his narrow bed made of steel and stared at the ceiling, which was of a pale shade of white, similar to the block that covered the grave.
>
> . . .
>
> Suddenly he heard something moving in the courtyard and a new day glared deep inside him. He sprang up and approached the window. There was Samīḥa, the landlord's daughter, picking jasmine flowers from a tree planted near the window. He observed her with voracious eyes. Her black hair was hanging over her shoulders, and her eyes looked defiantly. She was standing on the tip of her toes trying to pick the jasmine from a high branch, which allowed Yūsuf to see her white thighs.[17]

Residents of the same building, Yūsuf and Samīḥa engage in a complicated love relationship. Their conversations and encounters are surreptitious and characterized by an inescapable fear of being discovered by Samīḥa's family, who would not approve of their relationship. Patriarchal tradition and class differences hinder the love story between Yūsuf and Samīḥa: the former is a factory worker estranged from his family for sleeping with his brother's wife Faṭma; the latter is the daughter of a nouveau riche, the owner of the building whose basement Yūsuf currently occupies. Their relationship and the obstacles that it faces function as the point of departure for the exploration of the protagonist's inner universe and his reality of alienation and solitude. The female protagonist Samīḥa is but one of the elements of his desires, something Yūsuf is deprived of, just as he is deprived of light by his damp basement, and of freedom by his superior at work. Through the stream of consciousness the narrator brings together a variety of elements symbolizing the protagonist's alienation and desire for freedom, love and death.[18] The narrator constructs these parallels through a style that attaches specific connotations to the characters of Samīḥa, her father and the owner of the factory where Yūsuf works. Colours in particular possess a strong dimension functioning as elements of contrast between life and death, affluence and poverty, freedom and oppression, love and aloneness. While white, yellow and light colours in general symbolize life, marriage and freedom, black and dark colours suggest exploitation, death, solitude and poverty. The descriptions of Samīḥa's body and of the feelings her presence elicits are characterized by whiteness, lightness and a connection with the white jasmine and the sun.

> The sun was about to set. Samīḥa stood there for a while, immersed in the yellow light of the sunset, then she bent down and said: 'isn't the sun beautiful?'
>
> To his eyes Samīḥa looked somehow linked to the sun and the white jasmine. She was remarkably attractive, in such a way as though the scent of jasmine condensed and materialised in the form of white, hot flesh.[19]

Similar colours employed to highlight the connection between death and poverty can be found in the symbolic commonalities between his basement and the grave that Yūsuf sees at the funeral. Furthermore, the denunciation of class segregation and sexual deprivation is rendered through contrasting symbolisms and the hierarchical position between Yūsuf's basement and Samīḥa's family flat situated above his on the ground floor. Shifting frequently between a nameless third person narrator and Yūsuf narrating his story himself in the first person, the narrator coalesces the different elements that make up an oppressive reality. Female characters still possess a significantly reduced degree of agency and do not actively shape the protagonist's masculinity, which is defined by the patriarchal family (his and Samīḥa's) and by his working-class background, which prevent him from accomplishing his dream of marrying, having children and raising a family. The feeling of disparity between him and Samīḥa reaches a peak when the two eventually meet secretly in the basement at night, only to discover an incompatibility rooted in their differences, which ultimately reveals the impossibility of their love.

The crisis of masculinity in the stories of the 1970s

The two defeats of 1967 and 1973 (known in Syria respectively as *al-naksa*, Arabic for setback, and *Tishrīn*, October) marked a watershed for nationalist ideology in Syria and the wider Arab Middle East that denoted the beginning of a long period of crisis for the Pan-Arab ideology, a dream of unity that faded out, losing momentum and credibility.[20] In some respects, *Tishrīn* was the beginning of a new era for the Middle East, exposing Arab nationalist regimes' political inefficacy, and for Arab nationalism it marked the beginning of its decline. The 1970s began with the death of the Pan-Arab leader Jamāl ʿAbd al-Nāṣir and the Black September events in Jordan, when the Jordanian army clashed with Palestinian militias and expelled the Palestine Liberation Organisation. The disintegration of Lebanon in the civil war from 1975 onwards, and, finally, the recognition of the Israeli state by the Egyptian government in 1978 marked the end of a decade that undermined Arab nationalism and its emancipatory hopes almost irreversibly.[21] Yet, in the aftermath of the two Arab-Israeli wars, the sense of deep frustration and helplessness contributed to reinforce the power of militarized and authoritarian regimes like Assad's; regimes that in their rhetoric proclaimed the role of the leader as a manly combatant and promised to provide stability to a region that was profoundly traumatized by the Arab defeat of June 1967.

As Patrick Seale commented in his detailed biography of Ḥāfiẓ al-Assad, although politically catastrophic, the October War of 1973 marked the rise to prominence of Assad on a regional and national level.[22] While Arabic literature witnessed the emergence of a multiplicity of voices and themes, in the years following Ḥāfiẓ al-Assad's rise to presidency of the Syrian Arab Republic in the 1970s the revolutionary language of the Baʿath witnessed significant transformations. Especially after the 1973 war, the Syrian political vocabulary was enriched with familial metaphors, which in turn derived their coherence and intelligibility from the actual lived understandings of gender and power in Syrian families as patriarchal and male-centred. In the aftermath of the October War – celebrated by the Syrian regime as a victory – Syrian state propaganda started representing Assad as a national patriarch making explicit reference to his masculinity and manliness. Assad himself invoked manliness to refer to male protection and national defence.

Male characters had occupied the centre of most stories since Tamir's very first collection, but the more realistic tone and the evidently *engagé* style resulted in protagonists charged with great symbolic and heroic connotations, with little emphasis on sexuality and masculinities. With the 1970s the denunciation of alienation and privileges remains a central concern for this writer, but it is in this period that gender roles and sexuality come to the fore. In 'Arḍ ṣulba ṣaghīra' (A small hard earth)[23] the first signs of new and more complex masculinities emerge in the two protagonists' disquieting attitude towards the female body and sexuality, as well as in the connection between their sexual deprivation and eventual turn to homosexual desire. The story equals an ambiguous snapshot of a friendship-turned-love relationship, albeit portrayed through a timid allusion situated in the context of ethical sternness. The two protagonists, Aḥmad and 'Iṣām, share the same room as lodgers in the house of a widow, whose attractive body they enjoy peeking at from their room's window whilst she does the laundry. The boys get easily aroused at the sight of the landlady's uncovered thighs as she is engrossed in her work, ostensibly heedless of the boys' attention. The protagonists' sexual imagination, however, is not inspired by love and affection, or lust for the object of their desire, but by violence and forced sexual intercourse. They dream at length of creeping into her room at night and tearing off her clothes, of gagging her mouth and enjoying her immobility. The two boys' desire for the female body seems so strong that even the prospect of ending up in jail for rape does not seem to deter them from their plan, although it remains at the level of words. Once the landlady has completed the laundry, the two protagonists decide to leave the house. Yet, before emerging from their room Aḥmad thoughtfully knocks on the room door to warn the women in the house of their presence in order to cover themselves. As they leave the house the protagonists come across a pretty girl looking agitated, who suddenly disappears from their sight when a handsome man in fancy clothes pulls up in a car and takes her away. They then wander aimlessly through the city and wind up eating dinner together in a restaurant before returning to their lodgings.

> They returned home as the sun was about to set, and lay down next to each other on the same bed, while the other bed remained empty.[24]

The stark disparity between the heroic and manly gestures of the protagonist of 'Rabīʿ fī al-ramād' and the attitude towards women that men display in this story signal the beginning of a process of fragmentation and crisis. While this story does not explicitly depict a homosexual relationship, this subtext can be inferred from the story's closure, which clearly alludes at something more than a simple friendship. The absence of homosexual desire and same-sex intercourse in this period, and the timid reference to this theme in Tamir's early works remain in line with the general reticence of modern Arabic literature to address the subject. As it is hard to imagine that an insightful observer of his environment as Tamir might have been unaware of the reality of homosexual relationships, it is safe to explain this reticence – at least in the early period of his career – with the normalization of male-female sexual relationships that modernity brought about in the Middle East. While, on the one hand, in classical Arabic literature the theme of male homosexuality was pervasive, contemporary fiction, on the other, tends to obscure its nature and usually employs same-sex relationships to express malaise and decay.[25] In this story, the structure and imagery reinforce an idea of same-sex intercourse as a sign of disquiet, exemplified by the morbid approach to sex of the two protagonists, by their social alienation as well as by the coincidence between the two boys' retreat to their bed and twilight, an image often used by Tamir to connote violence and humiliation.

This and other stories of the same period capture a sense of male vulnerability and weakness, a process of questioning masculinity that has become characteristic of Tamir's works. A different approach to masculinity and patriarchy also appears manifest in new forms of resistance to paternal authority, culminating in the act of parricide. If on one hand in the very early excerpts quoted earlier in this chapter the father/son relationship is articulated through a less symbolic and more realistic killer/victim dichotomy, the 1970s mark a transformation in Tamir's style that subverts roles and responsibilities, refusing, even just by representing it, to accept the logic of patriarchy.

In 'al-ʿĀʾila' (The family) from *Dimashq al-ḥarāʾiq* the protagonists, all members of the same family, stage a compact and very intense series of events that hint at the fragility of familial relations. In this collection, significant transformations in both style and content signal the maturation of the author's writing towards a more nuanced view of masculinity, patriarchy and authoritarianism, and a multifarious set of protagonists. Upon returning home 'Abd Allāh searches for his keys in his pocket but cannot find them; his back bent, and his legs shaking he knocks on the door and an attractive young woman whom he does not recognize, but who claims to be his wife 'Ā'isha, opens the door for him and invites him in. 'Abd Allāh looks at her in astonishment and asks to see his wife but is laughed at by a young woman claiming to be 'Ā'isha. Immediately after entering the house the protagonist witnesses his little son breaking his little sister's head with a hatchet for stealing his ball. In a surreal twist to a story where two different temporal levels seem to overlap, and in which the protagonist finds himself caught in an unknown world, the little girl suddenly comes back to life to humiliate him and his despair at her death. Instead of merely condemning the unaffectionate authoritarian father, the story represents an attempt at looking at the father-wife-son triangle from the point of view of the helpless father. While depictions of the father-son bond and of the oppression brought about by the former onto the latter tend to focus solely on the son and his individual plight and quest for emancipation, the father and his attempts to negotiate between the expectations of masculinity and his individual aspirations are usually overlooked.[26]

From several similar other stories, the family as a broader institution comes under attack, exposing it as a hypocritical social construct of appearances and false commitments. The connections between patriarchy and authoritarianism become more evident as a more active role, charged with clearer political connotations, is assigned to the children in contrast with the overwhelming presence of fathers in earlier stories. The protagonist of 'Lā . . .' (No . . .) is a nameless old man who sitting in his courtyard is dozing off half-dreaming of becoming a feared and respected king. Suddenly his seven sons walk into the courtyard carrying wood planks, hammers and a saw, awakening the old man who inquisitively asks them about their plans. The sons ignore their father and his reprimands until the old man falls asleep again and wakes up to find out that his sons have made him a coffin and decided to bury him alive.[27]

While in the very early realistic representations of honour killings, paternal violence and distrust amongst the members of the same family children and especially daughters are depicted as the helpless victims of an absurd traditional institution, condemned as the repository of hypocrisy, these two collections come as the turning point in the subject/object reversal of the characters. Bestowing agency onto the victimized children, and arming them with material weapons, the narrator overturns the logic of realism that represents 'reality' for the purpose of denouncing injustice. The subject/object swap between parents and children transforms patriarchal rule, which is still nonetheless the target of demonization, into the object of the offspring's revenge, exposing the subtle complicity between the male-centred family and submissiveness to authoritarianism. This hidden interplay between the alienating obedience demanded by fathers and helplessness in the face of political tyranny emerges from the list of accusations the children address to their father who 'taught the boys to kiss the hand that slapped them and to sleep when the tempest is raging'. Linking also sexual incapacity and political inaction (as they prepare the coffins the sons accuse their father: 'We turn into old socks at the sight of a woman's knee'), both consequences of emasculating paternal tyranny, this story denounces the family as the source of atomization and helplessness. Without considering the allegorical implications that could be inferred through mere speculation, for example interpreting the elderly father as an allegory for the dictator with the children playing the part of the youth in revolt, parricide is sufficient to clarify a political stance that views family uncompromisingly as a fundamental link in the chain that ties down the desire for emancipation.

Although devoid of references to the major events that consolidated the Assad regime's power throughout the years, exposing the family as the repository of disharmony and resentment challenges the certainties of the imagined reader, clarifying the 'structure of feeling' represented by the firm connection between patriarchy and authoritarianism. These representations achieve a multiplication of views and meanings, subverting the claims of patriarchal authoritarianism by empowering characters and putting the possibility of rebelling against patriarchy into action.

'Fī layla min al-layālī': The denouncing of the authoritarian state and the gendered dimension of oppression

In addition to the changing representations of the patriarchal family, the stories of the 1970s expose the relationship between the increasingly authoritarian state and the undermining of the male protagonist's masculinity and dignity. The surreal condition of helpless male citizens under the capricious rule of an authoritarian regime has been a central aspect of Tamir's writing since the outset, and the humiliating practices of the state upon the individual have remained paramount in his later stories too. The emergence and the recurrence of this theme in Tamir's early works must be situated in the context of the increasingly overwhelming presence of the state and the security forces in the lives of individuals in Syria after independence, a phenomenon in turn paralleled by the rise of nationalist and military regimes.[28] The late 1970s and the consolidation of authoritarianism are usually associated in Tamir's oeuvre with *al-Numūr fī al-yawm al-ʿāshir* and in particular with the title story of that collection, which in turn has come to be considered as Tamir's masterpiece for its allegorical representation of authoritarianism. The title story, however, illustrates only one aspect of his production in this period and the denouncing of authoritarian pervasiveness and strategies of domination assumes a variety of configurations. In fact, the collection contains stories with a stronger focus on arbitrary arrest, torture and humiliation, of particular historical significance in the context of the consolidation of Ḥāfiẓ al-Assad's authoritarian regime. In the realm of gender and the body in particular, the desire to tackle this issue presents important developments. In the stories of this period, masculinity begins to acquire new connotations and while on the one hand the authoritarian father exerts his patriarchal authority on his wife and children inside the household, on the other hand outside of the home the male protagonists become victims of state patriarchy and tyranny. The gradual disintegration of a strong masculinity comes frequently as the consequence of authoritarian and arbitrary practices performed by representatives of the state upon the male citizen.

Abū Ḥasan, the protagonist of 'Fī layla min al-layālī' (One night),[29] is a middle-aged man with a great sense of pride in the respect and consideration that he enjoys in his working-class community. (See Appendix 1.2 for a full translation of this story in English.) A man whose belief in his own integrity the narrator describes at length, putting particular emphasis on the relationship between the model of masculinity that he embodies and on his working-class, suburban background. With its focus on Abū Ḥasan's crossing from his suburban hometown to central Damascus for a casual stroll, this story also addresses inequality and segregation, exemplified in the urban population's contempt for the protagonist's complexion and thick moustache. The baffled and amused looks that two young girls direct to his thick moustache make Abū Ḥasan all the more satisfied with his appearance, which he considers the visible mark of his manliness. As he walks aimlessly through its fancy streets, his estrangement from the modern bourgeois city becomes manifest, especially in his reaction to the unusual manners men and women around him display, signalling the emergence of models of masculinity and femininity alien to him. In contrast, the narrator goes on exalting Abū Ḥasan's moral qualities and virtue, describing him as a true gentleman, almost from another era, embodying an idealistic model of masculinity that has the thick-grown moustache as its status symbol, elevating him almost to a mythical status. Particularly, the narrator succeeds in conveying the image of a gallant male protagonist with the composure of a true gentleman striking a balance between strength and sensibility, courage and compassion. The narrator intentionally idealizes the protagonist and indulges in the glorification of his integrity, outlining Abū Ḥasan's profile in a way that makes what follows all the more relevant and surprising for the reader. In a sudden turn of events, and to his great surprise and perhaps due to his appearance, Abū Ḥasan is accused by a woman on the street of stealing her handbag. He is taken to the police station where the story begins to address arbitrary arrest, torture and the emasculating practices of the police in a graphic and explicit language.

Abū Ḥasan's mythical figure gradually shrinks before the readers' eyes, as he becomes the victim of the urban population's discredit and discrimination, as he is beaten and humiliated by the police officers who take great pleasure in undermining his sense of self-esteem and his most incontrovertible principles. The gradual process of emasculation at the hands of the police continues with fierce beating and torture, including the infamous *bastinado* method of punishment, which consists in the severe beating of a person's soles. The petty crime he is accused of makes the police's reaction and punishment all the more grotesque and surreal, emphasizing the arbitrariness of the state's treatment of the individual.

The process of undermining and emasculation of the protagonist happens in the context of his estrangement from his rural environment and as a consequence of his aimless roaming in the city, a place embodying values in contradiction with the protagonist's semi-mythical virility. The relevance of this story resides in the gendered connotations that the narrator attributes to the denouncing of authoritarian practices. The degradation of Abū Ḥasan's masculinity signals the transition of this theme from a markedly realistic style exposing the state as the oppressor and the average citizen as a victim to a more mature fashion of representing oppression. Here, the denouncing of the same degradation is accompanied by the detailed characterization of the protagonist's personality, as well as by the exposing of the state's grotesque practices. The centrality of the male body and its emasculation at the hands of authoritarian regimes is particularly relevant in the late 1970s when this collection appeared at the time of the consolidation of a regime under which 'men themselves are targets occupying a feminine position in relation to the regime apparatus, which is clearly identified as masculine'.[30]

This feminization as a form of humiliation of the protagonist is exemplified perfectly by a passage in which after being subjected to intense beating and renouncing his inestimable moustache, Abū Ḥasan is forced to state that he is not a man. He is a woman. Abū Ḥasan's emasculation employs the gradual breakdown of the protagonist's self-image to deconstruct a conceptualization of patriarchal masculinity as ahistorical and unified, exposing it as a fragmented experience 'both commanding and impotent, heroic and cowardly, central and marginal'.[31] The humiliation the protagonist is subjected to exemplifies a process of interplay of gender with the arbitrariness of the authoritarian state transforming men from dominant to subordinate.[32] This story exposes the changing and varying degrees of privilege inherent to masculinity, particularly through the gradual collapse of the manly protagonist through his departure from his popular environment (*al-ḥāra al-sha'biyya*) and his crossing into urban territory first, as well as through his subsequent arbitrary arrest and ultimate humiliation in front of the chief of police. However, while these stories certainly demonstrate greater awareness of the multi-faceted reality of gender roles and represent successful attempts at deconstructing patriarchal masculinity, they remain anchored in a male-centred language. The role women play is almost exclusively that of a symbol, of an accessory to the male's subjectivity, or the repository of the male's honour, an aspect that will be analysed in greater detail in Chapter 3.

Conclusions

This chapter has examined changing representations of masculinity and patriarchy in Tamir's early works, situating them in the territory of modernism, nationalism, ideological fragmentation and authoritarianism. Although they do not possess a strong ideological connotation, multiple examples from Tamir's debut on the literary scene display thematic and formal elements that allow us to associate them with the *ḥadāthī* mood, a trend that was organic to the nationalist and socialist emancipatory discourse rampant in Syria and in the Arab Middle East. In Tamir's early works, the overwhelmingly predominant presence of male protagonists and the marginality and objectification of female characters testify to deep-seated patriarchal connotations within Arab nationalist discourse. Tamir's early stories, particularly those published in the late 1950s and early 1960s, exemplify this inextricability between the representations of male protagonists and the predominant nationalist and emancipatory tone with its quest for sacrifice and destruction.

The stories in question were shaped by the transformations that cultural production in the Arab East witnessed across the 1960s and 1970s, which can be ascribed largely to the historical events of those years: the rise and fall of totalizing emancipatory ideologies charged with male-centred connotations, the defeats and decisive blows to these beliefs, as well as the rise and consolidations of authoritarian, invasive regimes. While the stories of the 1960s reflect the organic relationship that cultural production entertained with nationalist, socialist and emancipating political thought, the mid-1960s brought about the first signs of a more nuanced and multifarious view of masculinity and patriarchal tradition. The higher degree of unity that most stories enjoyed and the organic relationship between these works and the modernist *consensus* entail significant implications for the representations of male and female characters, a dimension that gradually changed in the stories of the late 1960s and early 1970s, later collected in *al-Raʿd* and *Dimashq al-ḥarāʾiq*.

In Tamir's early period the tight relationship between the *ḥadāthī* thought and literature, as laid out by Abu Deeb, manifested itself in male characters who were both heroic agents of destruction and change and helpless victims of patriarchal authority. Tamir's writings transitioned from a realist style that denounced sexism and the family as the site of oppression and atomization to a more mature surreal strategy successfully articulating the relationship between patriarchy and authoritarianism. While patriarchal rule was often represented as undisputable and immortal in the earliest stories, as early as the mid-1970s the uncompromising rejection of patriarchal institutions developed into one of Tamir's most effective literary tropes. The turning point of this development is represented by the subject/object reversal between fathers and children that bestows agency to the children while challenging the centrality of the patriarch and subverting the double-edged logic of realism. In a society asphyxiated by the unquestioned authority of a dictatorial regime, whose structure and hierarchy in turn replicate the patriarchal family, the empowering nature of such stories resides in the potential they possess to imagine alternative and unthought-of possibilities and to upturn the systems of signification that patriarchal authoritarianism seeks to naturalize.

In contrast, the final part has analysed the transformations that characterize Tamir's *al-Numūr fī al-yawm al-ʿāshir*, particularly with regard to the gendered configurations that the denouncing of authoritarian practices acquired. The performance of violent and emasculating practices on helpless citizens at the hands of the authoritarian state exposes the duality of patriarchal masculinity as a form of political domination affecting women and men equally. The few excerpts quoted here are only apparently 'silent' to authoritarianism and its abuses but setting their characters and the relationship between them against the backdrop of the events in Syria in the 1970s reveals their subversive potential.

3

The modern female

Female sexuality in the stories of the '*ḥadāthī*' period until the 1970s

This chapter examines the implications of a more female-centred style as well as the original style and language of stories with an existentialist outlook on the individual present, exploring the ways in which they project a female point of view on patriarchy and female sexual desire. In particular, it brings into view stories expressing an anti-patriarchal stance from the point of view of female characters to examine the representations of the female body and of female sexuality in Tamir's stories, and their development in his early works of the 1960s and 1970s. Motivating this focus on female eroticism is the desire to scrutinize the socio-political value of this trope in the context of concurrent historical events of Syria, analysing its relevance in a patriarchal context. The analysis draws on a normative understanding of gender roles that considers female sexual drives as a source of instability (or *fitna* in Arabic), to determine the degree to which these representations transgress a patriarchal worldview, for the privileged position men enjoy. This chapter also looks at the emergence of a pervasive and oppressive authoritarian state and its effects on the individuals to explore the role female characters possess as well as how the concepts of dominant, complicit and subordinate masculinity emerge through the representations of female characters.[1]

Neopatriarchy and the role of the female

Feminists and progressive thinkers in the Arab world and elsewhere have widely studied the intertwined relationship between authoritarianism, gender and patriarchy. The way nationalist and supposedly secular ideologies have dealt with women's sexuality has often been contradictory.[2] On the one hand nationalist and progressive forces have pursued a secular and socialist agenda, encouraging women's participation in social and political life; on the other, the degree of emancipation and equality the modernizing enterprise has achieved has been the subject of discussion.[3] That same modernizing enterprise reproduced the gender hierarchies, patterns and power relations of traditional patriarchy that it sought to defy, reinforcing a patriarchal conceptualization of the female's role as mother and of her sexuality as confined to its reproductive function.[4] This contradictory approach has resulted in a continuation of the traditional institutions that the modernizing and progressive ideologies of its foundational period sought to overthrow through modernization.[5] Narrowing the focus to look at Syria specifically, the institutionalization of feminism and gender equality embodied by organizations such as *al-Ḥaraka al-Niswiyya* (Women's movement) reproduces similar hierarchies and power relations between genders as it remained a state-controlled institution practising state feminism.[6] After all, this sort of trajectory is common to a variety of post-colonial contexts, and post-colonial nationalist and anti-imperialist movements and governments have often failed to answer the question of women and their emancipation.[7]

After independence, Syria witnessed the modernizing and usually authoritarian efforts of the Baʿath party, which were essential to the empowerment of women and to their access to education and public life and aimed, amongst other things, at incentivizing the participation of women in the public sphere, to achieve a clear break from the traditional patriarchal society. However, women's emancipation was an organic, but vastly subordinate, aspect to the country's modernization project.[8] The Baʿath's modernizing and emancipatory nationalist project was not devoid of contradictions and shortcomings, and a largely neopatriarchal language that assigned to women the role of mothers and bearers of the nation – which in turn is represented as a woman – has typified the Syrian Arab nationalistic discourse since the early days of the party, for example, in the writing of ideologues such as Zakī al-Arsuzī. Of particular relevance is the stress al-Arsuzī put on to the shared etymological root of the words *umm* (mother) and *umma* (nation), and on the nation as a mother to be loved and protected. This after all was common in colonial and post-colonial Arab contexts, where the nation is usually represented visually as a woman.[9] In particular, the association between Palestine and the female body usually allegorized the former as the occupied Arab land through images of rape and violation. In the collective imagery of nationalist propaganda, men, and especially leaders, are fertile and powerful defenders of the nation's honour against traitors and invaders.[10]

Tamir's works from the 1960s and 1970s reflect to a large extent the male-centred nature of the *ḥadāthī* project as well as the marginal and instrumental role of women. In the recurrent description of alienated individuals who cannot attain their basic necessities that characterizes this early period, women come across as passively subjected to the needs of men. Men dominate this landscape, with women usually relegated to play the role of accessories to the male protagonists' aspirations of bread, love and freedom. Men who suffer from material and intellectual deprivation recur considerably more frequently as the central motif of Tamir's earliest collections, which appeared in the context of modernism and social realism and were strongly influenced by the emancipatory ideologies of nationalism and socialism. Hunger, unemployment, hostility, violence, backwardness and ignorance lay as plagues upon his main characters, a grim picture that leaves women aside, confining them to the part of the victims of the victims.

'Thalj ākhir al-layl': The role of female characters in the struggle against the patriarchal family

The subtexts that had typified the Arabic modernist cultural production include a decisive rupture with the past and with tradition, identified usually, but not exclusively, with patriarchy. Novels, short stories and poems characterized by love, violence, tenderness, death, purification and destruction, as necessary to achieve the breakthrough to modernity and to reach a freer future, are the trademark of the literary movement that was organic to the *ḥadāthī* political project.[11] Many of these characteristics are central to Tamir's early works, in particular in *Ṣahīl al- jawād al-abyaḍ* and *Rabīʿ fī al-Ramād*, whose stories express a more manifest political commitment to the struggles of the marginalized sectors of urban society. Here, patriarchy and the unyielding authority of familial institutions join the state and religion to form the triangle of oppression that prevents the individual from expressing himself freely. The general feeling of estrangement that Tamir's characters usually experience often comes as a consequence of the inflexibility of familial traditions, and of the conformity that is demanded by parents. A quasi-anarchist impulse seems to animate the ferocious attacks on fathers and on the family in the early writings of this writer's career. From the numerous stories set in a familial context, and from the recurrence of stories, which amounts almost to an obsession with the household and its dynamics and repercussions on the individual, we can detect the extremely negative connotations assigned to the family as the primary societal source of identification. Oppressive fathers as the embodiment of ancestral tradition emerge as the main target of a style in which the family represents the first and most natural of the institutions that subjugate the individual in his or her quest for material and intellectual well-being. A deep sense of malaise surrounds the house, an asphyxiating feeling of being observed, watched, followed and patronized by an ever-present figure that expects unwavering obedience.

'Thalj ākhir al-layl' (Snow late at night) describes the internal conflict of the male protagonist Yūsuf, a young boy whose father has ordered him to find his wandering sister and kill her ('like a dog!').[12] The disparity between the father's obstinate conformation to unwritten rules and Yūsuf's genuine love for his sister functions as the narrative tool to denounce the patriarchal family as the site of incomprehension and atomization. In the realistic tone that characterizes such early works, one detects an underlying denouncing of honour killings and the interplay between traditional justice and state law. Love as the antidote for the unquestionable power of traditional institutions in this early stage represents a rudimentary weapon in the hands of the urbanized individual torn between modernity and tradition. Although devoid of any explicit sexual connotations, this story – which appeared in the early 1960s – is populated by symbols and allegories that emphasize the desire for liberation from the overwhelming institutions of patriarchy: the protagonist associates the catastrophe of his escaped sister with the presence of a snake living in his father's house's patio.

In the oppressive atmosphere created by the parents and the latent snake as embodiments of patriarchy, the protagonist Yūsuf finds refuge only in his imagination: he pictures the time when spring will come and he will finally find his sister, meeting her by coincidence in the city market. She will have moved on in her life and settled with the man she loves and Yūsuf will come home to 'find the snake tossed in the patio, dead and cold, and he will look at his gloomy father in triumph'.[13] His reconciliation with his beloved sister whom his father asked him to slaughter signifies the definite annihilation of patriarchy symbolized by the snake that the father in turn cherishes. Yet, this remains at the level of mere imagination, leaving the protagonists helpless in their quest for love and emancipation. The story contains no sexual dimension, and the frustration Yūsuf and his sister feel towards their father focuses on a vague atmosphere of oppression inside the family, embodied equally by the two parents. Although the narrator bestows some degree of agency on the runaway sister through her deliberate divorce from the patriarchal household, in most stories from this period the female protagonists are left at the margins of the narration and never address the high-minded social and political subjects that represent the author's main concern. After all, the sister remains in this story a nameless character, who does not enter the text except through the father's mention of the shame she brings upon the family, or through Yūsuf's imagination, leaving male protagonists at the centre of events.

'al-Ughniya al-zarqā' al-khashina' and 'Qaranfula lil-asfalt al-mut'ab': The objectification of the female and the emergence of female sexual desire

An overwhelming presence of male protagonists distinguishes Tamir's very first collection, *Ṣahīl al- jawād al-abyaḍ*. The narrator tells most stories in the first person, usually putting great emphasis on the male protagonists' suffering and discomfort at material and spiritual deprivation, at the lack of freedom in the patriarchal household, at their material poverty and at their sexual frustration. The impetus to denounce a collective reality of social inequality as well as to express strictly individual concerns come together in numerous stories, set mostly in the Syrian capital Damascus, Tamir's native city (recognizable in the title of one of the stories 'Rajul min Dimashq' (A man from Damascus) as well as in places like Baghdad Street, or the al-Ḥijāz Station). The concern with social issues such as industrialization, rapid urbanization, unemployment and inequality figuring prominently in a story like 'al-Ughniya al-zarqā' al-khashina' (The harsh blue song) reduces women to becoming an accessory in a broader picture dominated by male protagonists.

The only female character makes her appearance in the male protagonist's fantasy, who dreams of the day when he will become a king. In the following conversation the nameless protagonist describes to Abū Aḥmad, the owner of the local coffee shop, the ideal of the woman that he would like to marry.

> I will marry a woman that I saw some time ago on the street. A true woman. Her face was like the moon, framed by her black hair hanging loosely. Green eyes. Firm breasts that shuddered at every slightest movement of her body. I walked behind her for a while, and I enjoyed observing her behind as it quivered. Oh, what a woman! She was a big happy world! I will give an order to search for her and I will marry her. [14]

The evident objectification of the woman by the protagonist remains an exception in Tamir's oeuvre, which nonetheless especially in this first collection, contains several images of idealized women as the object of frustrated male desire. The focus on the individual's contemplations, showcased sometimes through the stream of consciousness, repeatedly stresses the lack of love amongst the protagonist's biggest concerns. Notably, most protagonists come from working-class, uneducated backgrounds, struggling to make ends meet and unable to find a woman with whom they can settle down. They usually idealize the woman they are looking for, a woman whose features match the popular (*sha'bī*) standards of beauty: long black hair, green eyes, fair skin tone.

As seen in Chapter 2 these stories explore the isolation and disenfranchisement of the protagonists giving prominence to men, bringing to the stage women with very little agency, merely as the object of male desire. Although Tamir's hero's highest aspiration is not sex per se but marriage and sentimental love with a soulmate he cannot find, for one reason or the other, the narrator makes the first timid references to eroticism, hinting at sexual intercourse between the protagonist and the city's prostitutes. A rich and suggestive language characterizes the stories of this period whose main themes remain inequality, poverty and deprivation, as experienced from the point of view of the male protagonists. The female body remains the object of the male protagonist's lust, described through suggestive representations and analogies which have become Tamir's signature style. The narrative structure frequently relegates the woman to helplessness and relative marginality, sometimes through allegories associating the female body or the sexual act of love with music or nature.

However, on a closer look, even in the early 1960s, Tamir's stories exhibit a more nuanced style and a different narrative angle in their dealings with sex, and in the exploration of the female body. It is in this period that the first original, albeit rare, representations of female eroticism appear, infrequent but nonetheless relevant because of the transgressive point of view on sexuality and desire that they propose. Few but relevant examples signalling the gradual emergence of sexual appetite as an urgency affecting the female too, emerged from a mass of stories whose protagonists seem bound to a vision of the woman as a marginal actor in the personal accomplishment of the male. At a significantly early stage in Tamir's very first collection, the first seeds of a preoccupation with female sexuality, a central theme in his later works, show a boldness of language that explicitly condemns families and social mores imprisoning desire and lust. Crucial to this process of concealment and repression is again the patriarchal family, embodied equally by mothers and fathers, who strive to protect the honour and the reputation of the household.

'Qaranfula lil-asfalt al-mut'ab' (Carnation for the tired tar)[15] is a brief sketch with four episodes occurring apparently in the same city, like a series of random snapshots with no apparent connection to each other. The first one is particularly significant as it frames an adolescent girl lying on her bed, her eyes closed, listening to a music that 'sent a dazzling and strange joy to her', 'her body lying on the bed cover was as mature as aged wine', 'without a man her body was like a sea, whose brown waves were sleeping'.[16] The protagonist finds herself alone dreaming, but suddenly the ever-present mother appears, to remind her of the deceitful nature of men who 'worship women as long as they smell their odour, but they desert them when their lust is quenched'.[17] Suddenly she remembers the story that her old neighbour told her once of a woman who was kidnapped by seven men, and only escaped their hold after several nights. In a poetic crescendo of the girl's imaginary depiction of the men around her and of their comments, her own imagination arouses her, and she begins to tremble and moan with pleasure. Yet, at the climax of her self-elicited enjoyment, she hears her mother's voice calling her insistently.

The seven men disappeared. She opened her eyes and said to herself:

- 'I'll be happy when my mother dies.'[18]

This story appeared as early as 1960, articulating the conflict between the traditional authorities of family and patriarchy, and the sexual desire pulsating inside men and women. An intolerant environment corners and represses the young protagonist's desires, but the latter's response to this asphyxiating situation remains at the level of words and masturbation. Devoid of the tyranny usually embodied by fathers but almost equally detrimental, the relationship between mothers and daughters/sons is also cast in a bad light. Tamir's female characters also come under the attack of his irony as complicit in an environment typified by fear and terror that their misogyny and conformism contribute to perpetuate.

'Wajh al-qamar' and 'Imra'a waḥīda': The emergence of the female point of view

Two stories in particular encapsulate the emergence of a more original female point of view: 'Wajh al-qamar' (The moon's face) and 'Imra'a waḥīda' (A lonely woman) published in the early 1960s in local literary magazines, and later included in *Dimashq al-ḥarā'iq* in 1973. These stories' relevance resides in their capacity to bring together a variety of themes to offer a taboo-breaking outlook on female sexual desire. The repression of sexual desire is strictly connected to patriarchy, misogyny, poverty, social disenfranchisement, religious hypocrisy and violence, as part of the broader struggle for individual emancipation that typifies the stories of this period. It is also significant how the pleasure that the protagonists of these stories experience through the discovery of their sexuality also denounces the oppressive presence of men in women's sexual life.

In particular, the way 'Wajh al-Qamar' (The moon's face)[19] articulates the oppressive but not invincible nature of patriarchy as a major obstacle to the free expression of the female's sexuality is the most relevant exception in the male-centred trend of the early collections. This story revolves around the protagonist Samīḥa's recollection of a series of experiences of sexual abuse, in parallel with her first moment of genuine awareness of the nature of her heterosexual desire. The story also presents a subject/object reversal that, contrary to a trend typified by parricide in the stories of this period, is careful not to alienate the man/father as the oppressor. The narrator portrays the protagonist's awareness of her sexual drives as blurred and uncertain, inarticulate and vague, but at the same time as an unstoppable and inexorable process of inner discovery and emancipation, which culminates with the collapse of the symbols of her upbringing. The reasons why the author did not publish this story in his compilations before 1973 are not strictly relevant in this context, and there is nothing to substantiate the idea that the sexually charged language might have encountered some disapproval from the publishers earlier in the 1960s. The deep glance that the narrator offers into the protagonist's inward-looking experience, articulated through the recall of her formative experiences, and paralleled by the distress the environment brings about, form a powerful and expressive assemblage.[20]

As Husam al-Khateeb recounts in what remains the only analysis of this story in English, the individual experience of the protagonist draws the reader into the exploration of the broader subject of sexuality in society.[21] Samīḥa's persona and her record of encounters with men from inside and outside her family, although apparently an inexorable series of inevitable abuses, bestows centrality to the sexual experiences of the female character to exemplify the asphyxiating nature of the patriarchal family. The glance into Samīḥa's confused and inarticulate desire includes the middle-aged rapist as someone into a sequence of men that Samīḥa, in a way, has *loved* and that has shaped her experience until this moment. The protagonist's longing for a renewed encounter with the same middle-aged man that raped her as a little girl (but still the only one able to satisfy her desire) provides an unidealistic view on female sexuality that steers away from the patronizing and objectifying tone of the very early stories.

For the first time this story passionately proposes a narration structured around sexuality as a fundamental need for women against the hindrances erected by men and misogynist patriarchy. Samīḥa's own imagination, illusions and fantasies suggests the inevitability of defeat for patriarchy and sexism, represented by Samīḥa's father, and by the middle-aged man, all of which signal the protagonist's unmanipulated quest for sexual fulfilment. Although somehow gruesome and disturbing, the protagonist's attraction to the same men who abused her as a twelve-year-old reinforces an element of autonomy in her sexual desire. The process through which Samīḥa comes to realize, accept and assert her sexual desire is beset by men and women equally as she receives a premarital and misogynist briefing from experienced women in her family.

The subject/object reversal addressed in the previous chapter returns here from the point of view of women. The exploration of Samīḥa's inner distress takes the reader on a journey into the psychological consequences of this worldview and of patriarchal impositions and prejudice. What is apparently only a close-up of the protagonist in fact possesses great social implications, manifest in the structure of the story, particularly the parallel relationship between the array of characters that populate the landscape of Samīḥa's daily experience: her father monotonously hitting a lemon tree with an axe and a madman's intermittent shouts that she hears from outside her window in her bedroom. Another parallel relationship is represented, on the one hand, by the madman's and Samīḥa's own libido, and on the other hand, by society represented by the children, the grocer, the barber and the father, who all violently condemn Samīḥa's and her objective correlative, namely, the madman. The female protagonist becomes aware of her sexual drives, of her desire to have sexual intercourse, thereby deconstructing the male's presence as besetting, finding comfort in her own sexuality through a journey of self-discovery that remains largely autonomous although confined to the limited space of her bedroom. The disparity between the closure, with Samīḥa ultimately finding gratification, and her previous, unsuccessful sexual encounter with the divorced husband highlights again the defectiveness of a misogynist idea of sexual intercourse as a necessity of the male exclusively. This value system implicitly views the physical act of love as an obligation the female must perform to fulfil the male's bodily urgency, but it is perpetuated in this story by misogynist women and not exclusively by men.

The structure of the story in other words deconstructs a binary male patriarchy versus female sexuality logic. The process of deconstruction is evident not only in Samīḥa's journey of self-discovery but also in a number of contradicting elements showing the multiple configurations of patriarchy and the possibility of emancipation: the felling of the lemon tree as the symbol of the protagonist's childhood happens at the hands of the father, not necessarily 'a typical oriental despotic father',[22] the fundamental role women play in the protagonist's family in trying to shape a self-erasing view of female sexuality and the considerable degree of attraction that Samīḥa feels for the middle-aged man to whom she 'looked with anxious longing . . . after she had waited long for him'. The middle-aged smelly man remains the object of her distorted desire until the definitive break with the past, after which she could finally articulate her desire for the crying madman, the other outsider figure in the story who is simultaneously the object of the protagonist's desire and the embodiment of her unconventional personality.

The overbearing role patriarchy plays in women's sexual lives appears mixed with religion in 'Imra'a waḥīda' (A lonely woman). The protagonist of the story Aziza ('Azīza), described as 'a beautiful young woman who was frightened of black cats', has turned to Sheikh Sa'id (Shaykh Sa'īd) to help her find her runaway husband, whose family intends to marry off to another woman. The word *sheikh*, an Arabic term used also in the Syrian vernacular to define someone with a high level of formal religious education, often extends to those who do not have such expertise but enjoy the respect and the reverence of the community for their age and experience. As Aziza explains her situation to the sheikh, his intimidating figure and the smoky atmosphere he creates with incense contribute to increase her helplessness.

> His eyes were two pieces of savage blackness, that encompassed Aziza, who was trying to escape from a terror that was very gradually increasing, while the smell of the incense that rose from a brass container filled her nostrils and slowly numbed her flesh.[23]

The first passages serve to characterize Aziza as poor and ignorant, a vulnerable personality that the sheikh understands as easy to manipulate for his own benefit. Sheikh Sa'id offers his services to help Aziza, who is alone and poor, to be reunited with her husband. But after conducting a brief interrogation with her, he concludes that her husband's family have put a spell on her and he offers to break it with a piece of incense for the cost of ten liras. Once he has extorted the money from her, the sheikh proceeds to break Aziza's spell, for which he needs to resort to the jinn, supernatural beings of Arab folklore as well as Islamic mythology. 'My brethren the djinn are kind. You will be lucky if you gain their love. They love beautiful women. Take off your wrap.' He says to Aziza.[24]

The story's language and style serve to construct an atmosphere that attaches extremely negative connotations to the sheikh. It uses smoke and darkness to symbolize obscurantism and superstition, exposing his greediness and lust, which contradict the authority that the sheikh enjoys and the confidence he inspires, and his cunning exploitation of the protagonist's faith and naïveté for his own pleasure and enjoyment. He starts by rubbing Aziza's forehead and face with his rough and large hands, which remind her of her father; then he grabs her neck, reminding her of her husband's soft and flabby hands. He strokes her breasts and 'the rest of her body' and then asks

Aziza to undress completely. Her refusal to undress, and her recollection of past negative experiences project the reader into Aziza's inner universe, and her aversion to pleasure which, similar to Samīha's in 'Wajh al-qamar', finds in the image of a screaming madman its objective correlative. She suddenly remembers a man screaming 'like a wounded animal on the ground, white foam on his mouth, moving his arms and legs like someone drowning'.[25] Aziza struggles and attempts to curb her sexual drive, which reminds her of the madman, evoking the negative connotations attached to female sexual desire as a form of insanity. At this point the story, which so far has associated ignorance, poverty, gullibility and religion to outline the profile of the female protagonist as a victim of patriarchy and religious hypocrisy, takes a decisive turn to depict the sexual act. As Aziza abandons herself to the sheikh's embrace and gets naked, the language transforms and takes a turn towards the poetic and the evocative, reflecting the protagonist's feelings that sexual enjoyment elicits.

In the middle of the casual sexual encounter with the sheikh, Aziza remembers her previous sexual experiences. The recollection of the loss of her virginity in particular serves to highlight the paradox of marital sex as a painful and socially driven activity as opposed to the casual but enjoyable moment of intimacy with the sheikh. The contrast is exemplified through the reference to a traditional patriarchal convention: the exposure by her mother of a blood-wet tissue to the public following the wedding night as the sign of the bride's bleeding upon sexual penetration proving her hymen's material and her family's moral integrity.

Together with 'Wajh al-qamar' the story is also relevant as it provides the female point of view on sexuality, transforming Aziza's unfortunate occurrence into an enjoyable experience, thereby proposing a conceptualization of sex as a delightful activity for the female. The story describes the protagonist's arousal through metaphors from nature that contrast the harshness she has been subjected to in her previous sexual experiences. However, as with Samīḥa, the protagonist does not seem to possess a self-aware subjectivity. The narrator portrays her as seemingly devoid of any form of resolution outside religiosity and it is only through her husband's disappearance that she comes to discover sexual pleasure. In the closure it becomes clear how the encounter/incident with the sheikh has served as a moment of realization for Aziza who would otherwise have remained unaware of her sexuality.

In the context of the grand narratives of modernization to which social realism was organic, this story challenges the overpowering character of patriarchy, exposing religious hypocrisy (manifestly embodied by the manipulative sheikh), but also condemning popular beliefs and superstition. The story projects the low minded protagonist as the helpless victim of religious hypocrisy, contributing to the denouncing of past traditions and of a popular (*sha'bi*) brand of Islam. The sheikh's unscrupulous actions leave the female protagonist helpless but only from his own point of view as, in his patriarchal and backward universe, he does not contemplate the idea that Aziza might have taken pleasure in his superstitious scam. However, while the variety of strategies that the sheikh employs to take advantage of her body, his religious and patriarchal authority, the incense and the smoke, the violence and the superstitious beliefs do contribute to cast a negative light on him, ultimately the physical act in itself is presented from Aziza's point of view as devoid of any harmful connotations.

'al-'Urs al- sharqī': Female sexuality as critique of the patriarchal family

The similar fashion in which the two tropes of patriarchal oppression and female sexuality developed in Tamir's early stories mirrors concurrent transformations in Arabic literature since the 1960s, in particular with regard to ideology. While the early stories expressed a more manifest rejection of past traditions as well as a strongly individualist stance, in the early 1970s a polyphonic and more fragmented vision, for example on patriarchal authority in the family, began to emerge.

Al-Ra'd, published in 1970, brings this preoccupation forward towards a more female-centred narration but still exposing the severity of patriarchy and its male-supremacist and belittling attitude towards women. The story quoted later brings forward the concern with female sexual identity through a style that depicts traditional institutions such as arranged marriages coldly, but also uses elements of surprise and a gradually stronger female presence in the text. This constitutes a break with earlier representations of women as an accessory of the man's necessities. Ṣalāḥ and Hayfā', the protagonists of 'al-'Urs al- sharqī' (the Oriental wedding),[26] embody the two extremes the narrator uses to poke fun at the institution of arranged marriage: the former a young school boy who wants to get married, willing to accept whomever his parents decide for him; the latter the proverbial *bint al-jīrān* (the neighbours' daughter, the girl next door) an expression used in the Syrian vernacular to indicate an ordinary well-mannered girl perceived as familiar and dependant, whom Ṣalāḥ's parents choose for him as his future wife. The boy soon comes across as naïve and sexually inexperienced, but the prospect of marrying him to the neighbours' daughter leaves the father heedless to this fact.

> - 'And so you've decided to get married. You chose the right time of the year, because the winter is approaching', said the father. He coughed and rubbed his hands enthusiastically and added, 'How beautiful it is to fall asleep cuddling to warm flesh!' – 'I don't like to sleep with women' said Ṣalāḥ calmly.
>
> - 'Why do you want to get married then?' said his father in perplexity. [27]

Ṣalāḥ's and Hayfā''s parents eventually meet to discuss the details of the engagement, and agree on the price the boy's father must pay to obtain the girl's hand in marriage to his son. A great deal of irony and cold realism surrounds the two parents debating Hayfā''s price per kilo, exposing a tradition that excludes the girl from the decision-making process. In addition, the conversation between Ṣalāḥ and Hayfā' when left alone together in the living room would seem to suggest an accusatory tone, depicting the girl as helpless and accommodating, but is later revealed as an element in the build-up that takes the reader into the unexpected closure. At a first glance, the dialogue mimics a realistic depiction of a stereotypically submissive young girl, which in Syrian popular slang would be described as one 'whose lips no one but her mother has kissed',[28] and who holds no agency with regard to her sexuality and her future life. In reality, Hayfā' is more aware than what she might appear, and it is only in the closure that she shows all her maturity and sexual awareness in comparison with the boy's childish and insecure nature.

> Ṣalāḥ found himself compelled to get closer and stick his face to her naked breast. Then his mouth seized her nipple with a savage desire to swallow it. He did not eat Hayfā''s breast, instead he broke into tears, when her bosom did not grant him warm milk.[29]

The whole story is structured in such a manner as to build up the narrative tension, by employing characters from a traditional setting that readers are familiar with (like the well-mannered girl), using the element of surprise and Hayfā''s astute nature to undermine the patriarchal-perpetuator-versus-youn g-victim pattern. What seems to his parents a mature man, who kisses his father's hand in reverence, ready to officially enter manhood through marriage, is in reality a little boy whose infantilism is unmasked by Hayfā', presumably a naïve and essentially simpleminded character. The story revolves around Ṣalāḥ and his ineptitude to ridicule the institution of arranged marriage, yet it also gives prominence to women and their awareness of their sexual drives. The prominence the female gains comes at the detriment and ridicule of patriarchy and its customs, which the more assertive and self-confident attitude of characters like Hayfā' contribute to voice. At the level of language, the disregard for patriarchal institutions comes about through their ridicule in a build-up that expresses no judgements, but leaves it to the female protagonist to unmask the conventions through the assertion of her mature sexual desire.

'al-Ightiyāl': The rise of the authoritarian state and the objectification of the female body

As outlined in the previous chapters, the mid-1970s and 1980s inaugurated a new phase in Syria's political life. The progressive and emancipatory language of the Ba'ath party witnessed a regression paralleled by the broader retreat of Pan-Arab nationalism and socialism. A series of traumatic events that left indelible scars in the Syrian collective memory made European-style modernization and secularization lose appeal. Simultaneously, the consolidation of military authoritarianism entailed the spread of extensive surveillance and coercion that amounted to oppression. In addition to the institutions of punishment common to the modern state, the intimidation and suppression of all forms of political dissent became widespread in this period, affecting intellectuals as well as ordinary citizens. The intrusive and cancerous presence of the state in the life of citizens turned into a defining trait of society in Syria and in the wider Arab world, a monolithic institution characterized by arbitrariness and blind violence.[30] The efficiency of its security apparatus and of its intelligence agencies (*mukhābarāt* in Arabic) became the most advanced and functional aspects of the authoritarian state, depriving citizens of their private existence and making them prey to its capriciousness.[31] In Syria, since 1963, Emergency Law exempted the intelligence agencies from judicial checks, encouraging widespread practices of torture. In the aftermath of the ascension to power of Ḥāfiẓ al-Assad in 1970, the traditional *mukhābarāt* expanded their branches, building a reputation for brutality, violence and corruption amongst ordinary Syrians.[32] The themes of arbitrary arrest and the grotesque logic of the modern state's representatives appear in Tamir's stories as early as 1960; however, authoritarian violence on ordinary citizens becomes extensive in the mid-1970s, exemplified by the story 'Fī layla min al-layālī' (One night) analysed in Chapter 2, as well as by numerous other stories tackling authoritarian practices of domination published in the mid- to late-1970s and later included in *al-Numūr fī al- yawm al-'āshir* in 1978.

More generally, modern Arabic literature has addressed the issues of authoritarianism, foreign occupation and disenfranchisement through the extensive use of bodily metaphors. While the nation is frequently conceptualized as female, this stands in stark contrast with descriptions of the male's feminization and sexual incapacity as symbols of defeat, on one hand, but also of sexual prowess as embodied revenge on the Western colonizer, on the other. The political significance of sexuality and gender roles in Arabic literature and cinema characterizes the works of authors such as Najīb Maḥfūẓ, Ghassān Kanafānī and al-Ṭayyib Ṣāliḥ who made extensive use of sexual metaphors and similarly objectified the female body as the repository of the male's and the nation's honour. In Maḥfūẓ's *Zuqāq al-midaqq* (Midaq alley),[33] indications of male homosexuality made their first appearance in modern Arabic literature but the novel is notable for the allegorical embodiment of the Egyptian nation in the character of Ḥamīda, and her role as a prostitute who sells her body to a local pimp delivering local women to British soldiers in Cairo during World War Two.[34] In Kanafānī's *Rijāl fī al-shams* (Men in the sun), a group of Palestinians stranded in Iraq are smuggled illegally into Kuwait by a treacherous fellow Palestinian truck driver who lost his genitals fighting in the 1948 war.[35] A lack of manliness and low moral standards typify this character's personality, rendering a sense of betrayal and failure through his emasculation.[36] Muṣṭafā Sa'īd, the protagonist of Ṣāliḥ's *Mawsim al-hijra ila al-shamāl* (Season of migration to the north),[37] personifies both Sudan's experience of colonization, acculturation and migration at the hands of the

'North' (i.e. the imperialist Western colonizer), as well as the colony's 'revenge' on the 'North'.[38] Muṣṭafā Saʿīd carries out his revenge in London, inverting the traditional masculine role assigned to the colonizer and the feminine nature of the colonized, engaging almost obsessively in sexual intercourse with English women and leading them to commit suicide.

While most of Tamir's stories portray the confrontation between the state and citizens leaving women outside the picture, 'al-Ightiyāl' (the assassination)[39] is significant for the connotations attached to the female body as a token of the male's helplessness vis-à-vis the overwhelming force of nameless men who chase him inside his house and rape his girlfriend while he hides inside her body. Although the narrator makes no mention of the *mukhābarāt* or any other security branch, the rapists described by the narrator/protagonist as 'men that I don't know' can be easily associated with the arbitrary forces of state intelligence agencies.

Comparing this to the original female point of view of 'Wajh al-Qamar' and 'Imra'a waḥīda', which appeared as early as 1960 and 1962, respectively, makes it obvious that the development of this theme in Tamir's writing did not follow a coherent line of elaboration. In this story, published as late as 1978, the female body remains entangled in representations that assign a secondary role to it, usually for the purpose of symbolizing the male's success or demise, or to denounce social injustice. Behind its more manifest political significance, the narrative device employed to voice the angst at authoritarian arbitrary violence reveals an objectification of the woman, and her accessorial nature in a male-dominated environment. 'Al-Ightiyāl' has been praised as a courageous interpretation of the current state of 'domesticated societies'[40] for the way in which it exposes the overwhelming and unchallenged forces of authoritarianism and their practices of humiliation of the individual's dignity. However, the text employs images that ideally take us back to the early days of the realist representations of male protagonists, with their frustration and deprivation voiced through the marginalization of the female. Here, the female body is reduced to the role of the carrier, the accessory through which the authoritarian state performs its humiliating practices.

Deconstructing 'al-Ightiyāl' as an attempt to denounce and undermine patriarchal authoritarianism eventually reveals that the language of this attack remains entangled in the same male-dominated worldview that it seeks to undo. Here, the female body encapsulates the degradation of the man, becoming once again an accessory of his existence rather than enjoying its own autonomous experience. Although other stories of the same period suggest an acute awareness of female subjectivity and sexual desire, the penetration the nameless woman is subjected to at the hands of the thugs, and the man's consequent humiliation reveal a tendency to objectify the female body in the attempt to tackle the grotesque practices of the authoritarian state. The 'beloved' sacrifices her body to protect the male protagonist from the beating and the arrest, which in turn become a pretext for the thugs to abuse her. This objectification of the female body as the site of the male's honour and humiliation is mitigated by her greater endurance in the face of the antagonists. The male's emasculation materializes not only in the brutality visited upon his partner but also more specifically in his inertia and his passive following of the events as they unfold before him, and in the cowardice displayed by hiding inside his partner's body.

Conclusions

A chronological examination of female characters in Tamir's writing reveals the emergence of a more female-centred style. This includes explicit representations of female sexual desire from the perspective of women that are, from a very early stage in his career, greatly suggestive, and employ a poetical tone and stand out in Tamir's oeuvre. Yet, although significant in the prominence they bestow on the protagonists' inner needs and longing for sexual intercourse, most stories do not articulate the woman's experience as the norm but seem to merely strive for the destruction of the traditional patriarchal order. The noteworthy presence of suggestive sexual images, however, portrayed through metaphors of nature and the world of animals, indicates the author's preoccupation with the subject since his first appearance on the literary stage, and an openness to address sexuality and libido as a fundamental need for the individual in his or her quest for freedom and emancipation.

The evolution in the style of Tamir's representations of female sexuality in particular in 'Wajh al-Qamar' and 'Imra'a waḥīda' shows the first female protagonists exploring their own sexuality. In their representations of the female inner libido, and the relationship between her eroticism and the environment around her, these stories possess the verbal dynamism of an original and explosive mix of prose and poetry. The presence of a sexually aware and active female character emerges also in opposition to patriarchal tradition in 'al-'Urs al-sharqī', sarcastically attacking the institution of arranged marriages, while also putting forward the notion of female sexuality as enjoyable.

Examining the confrontation between citizens and the authoritarian state from the point of view of women has confirmed the predominantly male-centred character of stories with a more politically accusatory message. In the 1970s the increased presence of widespread violent practices in most stories reflects the rise and consolidation in Syria of an authoritarian regime with a pervasive role in the lives of citizens. The urgency to address this issue results in a form of objectification of the female that leaves intact the essentially male-centred nature of the works of this period.

4

From object to subject

Multiplicity, transgression and the sexualization of the female

This chapter situates the analysis of female sexuality in Tamir's latest stories in the context of the collapse of the totalizing and unifying ideologies which began in the 1970s and coincided with the germination of marginal narratives proposed by Abu Deeb. This chapter proposes an interpretation of this process of disintegration as constitutive for the germination of an original style that engenders multiplicity and allows for the emergence and flourishing of a new feminine subjectivity that stands in stark contrast with the predominantly male-centred structure of the early period. This multiplication of voices and viewpoints is exemplified by dynamic conceptualizations of masculinity and patriarchy, as well as by transgressive representations of female libido that challenge the conceptualization of female sexuality as reprehensible.

The stories analysed in this chapter were published between 1994 and 2002, which in Tamir's trajectory represent his first literary output after sixteen years of literary 'silence' following his self-imposed exile from Syria to England. The analysis looks at how the ever-present, assertive and dominant female protagonist in Tamir's latest works is illustrative of a new prototypical female, embodying a break with a traditional form of representing women, transgressing the standard social codes of honour, shame, tradition and patriarchy. The relevance of the taboo-breaking representations of sexuality resides in the subversive potential that sexual images possess in a patriarchal context where female sexuality and subjectivity contain considerable political implications.

'al-Bustān' and 'Sa-naḍḥak' as different approaches to oppression and gender roles

Since his very beginning as a short-story writer, Tamir's works have dealt with sexuality extensively, mostly projecting sex as an enjoyable experience. In contrast to a predominantly marginal role female characters played in the stories of the early period, in Tamir's latest works the female protagonist progresses from playing the role of the object of male desire to becoming a subject that gains centrality and agency. A stronger emphasis on her sexual desire bestows the female with supremacy in her relationship with the male. A comparison between the different roles women play in his early and latest stories highlights this disparity: While in the early collections women are marginal or accessorial objects in a male-centred society or objectified by the narrator to emphasize the humiliating practices of the authoritarian state, in his latest works the male and female protagonists are represented in a more equal manner that is evident in both the language and the style. This development is manifest in the roles performed, as well as in the more uniform linguistic registers employed to describe male and female characters.

The two stories quoted later in this chapter, taken from collections that appeared in very different historical contexts, illustrate the transformations in the representations of the female body that typify the latest period of Tamir's career. They can be read as two versions of the same story as seen from two different angles with a different approach to the sexes. In 'al-Bustān' (The orchard) – published in 1971 – the narrator begins by employing elements of magical realism to introduce the two protagonists, Samīḥa and Sulaymān, and their relationship.

> In the old days Samīḥa was a fish that lived in the sea, then she turned into a drop of water in a cloud, then one day Sulaymān met her, and she became a beautiful woman. He loved her mouth and her two fine lips, which gave out fire, music, wind, light and fire.[1]

The accurate and poetic description of the female protagonist's beauty, as well as the rain as a metaphor for sexual enjoyment, display the features typical of Tamir's early period and the tendency to associate elements of nature with the female body, emphasizing the disparity in the roles performed by men and women. While walking through the city, the two protagonists find themselves entering an orchard, and they dream of living the rest of their lives there. Samīḥa kneels down to put her ear to the ground and listens to the earth laughing. Suddenly, a group of four men interrupt their peaceful and idyllic conversation, moving rapidly towards them, carrying sticks in their hands. The thugs arouse Sulaymān's anger by asking him to share Samīḥa's body with them in a confrontational and provocative tone. As he tries to get away with Samīḥa the bullies knock him down and beat him, and they proceed to rape Samīḥa.

Published originally in 1971, this story can be understood in the context of a sense of disquiet engendered by the lack of individual freedoms that typified Tamir's very early works, but also as the expression of an urgency to denounce widespread violence and abuse that emerged prominently in the 1970s. As seen in Chapter 3, the combination of this necessity to address the increasingly pervasive presence of the state, together with a linguistic style emphasizing the disparity in the roles assigned to men and women, resulted in the objectification of the latter. This story too presents similar connotations attached to the female protagonist Samīḥa: she magically turns from a fish into a drop of rainwater (a frequent metaphor for sexual intercourse) and her violation at the hands of the bullies functions as the literary device to emphasize the male individual's helplessness.

Twenty-seven years later the title story of *Sa-naḍḥak*, published in 1998, presents a similar set of characters but with significant transformations in the roles assigned to male and female protagonists. The narrator and his beloved remain nameless but enjoy each other freely and blend in with the surrounding nature, or live through ordinary everyday moments, only to be disrupted in this case not by unspecified 'men carrying sticks' but by the police (*rijāl al-shurṭa*), who, however, are unable to unsettle the harmony of their love relationship. This time the story is narrated in the first-person plural voice, eliminating the boundaries between the two elements of the couple. The attack happens not on the man, on his masculinity and his honour, but on the couple as a dyad, establishing equality between the two sexes and no longer objectifying the female body as the repository of honour. In addition, however grim the feelings that the ubiquitous police might initially elicit as they descend on their house, wit, magic and imagination come to the couple's rescue. The title of the story itself (We shall laugh . . . we shall laugh a lot) expresses greater optimism and a defiant demeanour in the face of the asphyxiating presence of authoritarianism embodied by the police.

(1) One day the police descended upon our house, looking for me and my wife but they did not manage to find us because I turned into a coat rack and my wife turned into a sofa, and we laughed when they left the house in disappointment.
(2) Another day the sky was clear blue, so we went to a park, but suddenly the police raided the park looking for us. They didn't find us, because I transformed into a black crow whereas my wife turned into a green tree of many branches, and we laughed at their failure.
(3) One day my wife was tired of working in the kitchen, so we went to a restaurant, but as soon as we started eating the police surrounded the restaurant and stormed it with frowns on their faces, to conduct a thorough search, looking for us. They didn't find us because I turned into a knife, and my wife transmuted into a glass of water, and we laughed a lot when they left the restaurant in despair.[2]

Magical realism in this instance serves not as a tool to romanticize the female as a delicate object but as a strategy to poke fun at the grotesque practices of the authoritarian state and its blind victimization of both male and female characters equally. The political significance of a style that restages reality employing elements of the fantastic corresponds to the urgency to present the point of view of women and the disempowered vis-à-vis tyrannical powers.[3] Tamir has made use of this device since his early years as a writer; however, its significance in the context of this analysis lies in the different approach to the sexes that the text puts forward, going beyond the previous separation between man and woman that bestowed prominence and centrality on the former through the penetration of the latter's body. This story also expands the width of space allocated to the protagonists, emerging from the claustrophobic orchard where the thugs humiliated the male in the first story from which the protagonists were unable to escape to a variety of spaces and situations all meant to deride the victimizers. This expansion of settings becomes regular in Tamir's latest period, with female characters playing a new assertive role in diverse places and situations, seldom relegated inside the house or to their role as inactive housewives.

The postmodern short story and the emergence of the female point of view

The magical realist element of this story and its more equal approach to gender roles already figured prominently in Tamir's first 'exile' collection *Nidā' Nūḥ*, which was characterized by a greater thematic homogeneity in contrast with the fragmented structure of the stories. Most stories in this collection contain different sub-stories, with further sub-plots written in different styles and carrying different titles, a feature that Tamir began experimenting with in the late 1960s but which becomes systematic in *Nidā' Nūḥ* and *Sa-naḍḥak*. While female protagonists were the exception in the early stories from the 1960s and 1970s, *Nidā' Nūḥ* and *Sa-naḍḥak* present multiple signs of the fragmentation of the text as well as a much greater presence of female protagonists with an increased awareness of their sexuality. In *Nidā' Nūh* the thematic homogeneity is rendered through the intertextual restaging of elements of the Arab heritage, and through the reinvention of traditional functions as a device to put forward a multifarious perspective on present concerns to which gender roles are central. By way of illustration, 'Shahriyār wa Shahrazād' (Shahriyar and Shahrazad) restages the *One Thousand and One Night*'s frame-story, reversing the roles of the story-teller, assigned to the husband Shahriyār, and that of the king/queen to Shahrazād. While in the original collection of folktales Shahrazād told a different story every night to save herself from Shahriyār's misogynist wrath, in Tamir's the latter is the helpless victim of the queen's desire to be told stories 'that make me forget the concerns of my government, and the bitter and ugly truth according to which men are not loyal to their wives'.[4]

Although these excerpts do not necessarily possess a sexual dimension, their significance resides in the role female protagonists specifically play as well as in the broader stylistic transformations that the stories present. Such transformations can be interpreted as a reaction to the breakdown of an old order, which in turn entailed the exploration of tradition in search of what Stephen Guth calls 'undamaged treasures', that is, stylistic and thematic elements that could function as meaningful tools to address a changing reality.[5] Guth explains the new aesthetics of pleasure in Arabic literature of the 1990s and early 2000s as a process of 'digging in the ruins' of the 'collapsed house' that is modernity, a process of experimentation that allows for the emergence of a new conceptualization of desire detectable in the breaking of taboos and the increasingly transgressive representations of pleasure and the body.[6]

Similarly, drawing on the relationship between cultural production and ideological fragmentation, many have interrogated the emergence of a new approach to the female, as well as to sex, pleasure and gender-motivated fiction in the landscape of Syrian and Arabic contemporary literature that has emerged in Arabic literature in the late 1990s. This phenomenon is part of a broader new fashion of cultural production that germinated not only in Syria but in the broader field of cultural production in Arabic in the 1980s. The works of the Syrian novelist Rūzā Yāsīn Ḥasan and her representations of the body as a means of criticism of patriarchal authoritarianism exemplify a broader *nouvelle vague* of writers in Syria who have made a name for themselves by rejecting traditional literary culture, surpassing the idea of commitment and striving towards individualism, focusing on the individual and his/her struggle for freedom.[7]

'al-Maḥsūda': The development of the sexual trope and the process of self-realization of the female

The advent of the female protagonist's perspective in Tamir's latest collections marks the transition towards female-centred writing, witnessed on a larger scale in the 1990s. Sex does not recur in *Sa-naḍḥak* as frequently as in other collections, but the roles the female protagonists play in this collection signal the gradual emergence of their new subjectivity to the detriment of male protagonists and their masculinity. This development further contributes to the deconstruction of the binary logic of patriarchy, which places men over women hierarchically, and provides the female character with an authentic voice without idealizing her or proposing didactic views on women's emancipation. This gives centrality to the role of female sexual desire and libido specifically, and to the taboo-breaking nature of eroticism that is addressed openly from the point of view of women. The introduction of female sexuality into the narrative has, after all, affected male Arab writers such as the Syrian playwright Sa'adAllāh Wannūs as well, whose early plays usually voiced a strong commitment to the Arab nationalist cause. With the gradual retreat of Arab nationalism and of the modernizing project, Wannūs's 1990s plays, in particular *Ṭuqūs al-ishārāt wa al-taḥawwulāt* (Rituals of signs and transformations), exemplify the degree of fragmentation Arabic fiction and theatre reached in the last decade of the previous century.[8] This transformation has heavily affected Tamir's oeuvre as well, although in a considerably different fashion. While Wannūs's female hero asserts her autonomous identity and existence through violence, penetrating fiercely into the narration and depriving the male of his centrality, in Tamir's stories the female protagonist's sexual drives turns into a 'weapon' that allows her to symbolically defeat patriarchy and express her agency.

In 'al-Maḥsūda' (The envied woman) the environment in which women operate is still limited to the household, but the story introduces a new model of femininity and of active female sexuality that informs and shapes the masculinity of the male protagonists. At the breakfast table Izdihār informs her nameless husband that their neighbour Khadīja is pregnant in her fifth month, although her husband, also nameless, has been away for seven months. Although her husband advises her not to interfere in their neighbours' affairs, Izdihār goes to see Khadīja to ask her for an explanation, justifying her intrusion with a popular saying attributed to the prophet of Islam by which Muslims are expected to take care of their neighbours living up to seven doors away.[9] The saying evidently has very little to do with the protagonist's thirst for gossip, but serves to clarify the nature of the milieu in which the events take place, and to satirize Izdihār's resorting to religious beliefs for trivial purposes. In an unexpected turn, Izdihār finds out that Khadīja's husband visited her one night and passionately made love to her after missing her for a long time. Khadīja's description of her encounter with her husband elicits a feeling of envy in Izdihār who later confronts her own husband and relates to him the reality of their neighbour's pregnancy.

> - 'God the Almighty will judge us because we doubted our poor neighbour' – said her husband.
>
> - 'Envy is wrong' said Izdihār, 'but I must say I envy our neighbour Khadīja for her husband, who does not neglect his marital obligations, regardless whether he is at home or away'.
>
> Her husband lowered his head and did not try to look at his wife.[10]

This story introduces themes and roles that become central and considerably more frequent in the two following collections, *al-Ḥiṣrim* and *Taksīr Rukab*.

The centrality of the two female protagonists stands in contrast with the evident insignificance and lack of agency of the two male protagonists whose names the narrator does not mention but refers to them through periphrasis (Izdihār's or Khadīja's husband). This fashion of representing marital relations and their nomenclature contradicts the most widespread examples in Syrian society, in which a woman can sometimes be referred to as Mr. So-and-so's wife, but rarely the opposite.[11] Moreover, the female's capacity to intimidate and subjugate her husband derives from her judgement of his sexual performance and sexual prowess, which in the closure emerges in all its relevance inside the household. As the story unfolds and Khadīja's personality comes to the fore, we witness the gradual deterioration of the male's privileges, reversing the society's judgemental attitude towards Khadīja's immoral sexual relations into a condemnation of the male's incapacity to live up to masculinity and its expectations. The other protagonist, Izdihār, goes through a journey of discovery and self-empowerment the moment Khadīja crushes her standards of female respectability with an assertive account of her impregnation. Izdihār approaches her neighbour with a baggage of assumptions, with an almost *schadenfreude* attitude only to discover what Khadīja did, exposing her unhappy marital situation and her husband's evident sexual impotence. Highlighting the disparity between the different standards of masculinity and femininity as understood and performed inside the household or in public, the story exposes sex as the one empowering tool women possess to counterbalance the predominance of men in a patriarchal milieu.

The emergence of transgressive female sexuality in *al-Ḥiṣrim* and *Taksīr Rukab*

The pivotal transformation of the female's role in the realm of sexual desire happens more frequently and more openly in *Taksīr Rukab*. According to the author, 'breaking someone's knees' – or *taksīr al-rukab* in Arabic – is, in the parlance of the Damascene middle class, a metaphor for a long and exhausting sexual activity that literally 'breaks a man's knees'.[12] Tamir has explained the focus on sexuality in this particular collection with his desire to unmask widespread hypocrisy amongst Syrian religious figures.[13] The unfavourable opinion this writer maintains of the religious establishment emerges in this collection with an ironic stance that ridicules their connivance with power. Eros, marriage, affairs, sexual frustration and religious hypocrisy play a predominant role in nearly all stories. Similar to other titles in Tamir's career, this title too seems to carry a double meaning, and in addition to the sexual dimension the title also employs this painful image to refer to the destructive effects of authoritarianism on ordinary individuals.[14] From the very first page, rather than just picturing conventional erotic scenes, sexuality serves to upturn the traditional hierarchies and conventions of gender relations and bring together human, social, political and religious issues.

The following story – quoted in its entirety – epitomizes in a few lines the minimalist representations of female libido that traverse this collection, which represents the culmination of a theme, that of female sexuality and eroticism, that in this compilation finds its most eccentric representations.

> Lama was accustomed to dozing off and putting in her mouth whatever happened to be in her hand. Her mother advised her in an angry and reproachful voice to get rid of her nasty habit, especially now that she was engaged and about to get married. But after marriage Lama discovered that her mother was naïve and that her advice was wrong, for what she had grown used to doing while dozing was widespread, prized, and desirable.[15]

The explicit manner of addressing oral sex and its urgency forms a crucial part in the development of the representations of female sexuality that amounts to an obsession in this particular collection. Portrayed in a cold and condensed language, this collection achieves a crystallization of female sexual desire as the catalyser of events in practically all the stories. This new female protagonist already began to emerge in *Nidā' Nūḥ* and *Sa-naḍḥak*; however, while the stories of those two collections exhibited a fragmented style of writing, the sixty-three stories of *Taksīr Rukab* display a formal unity of theme and language in which sex becomes the leitmotif. Sex, in other words, is the 'undamaged treasure dug out of the ruins' that Guth refers to in his analysis of postmodern Arabic literature; its enjoyable and politically transgressive nature makes it a lasting theme that retains 'the quality of a reliable certainty in light of ideological breakdown and pessimism'.[16]

The stories are usually structured around two characters, a man and a woman, the former imprisoned in male-supremacist expectations and contradictions that demand he perform his 'natural' role, while the latter unmasks the insecurities behind the male's 'manly' behaviour. The self-confident nature of the female emerges through her fearless assertion of her sexuality which strips men of their phallic authority and disregards hierarchies to the detriment of the male's assumptions of physical supremacy. In the following story, a fashion of allegorizing the phallus with a knife, common in the stories of the latest period, serves to build up the narrative tension to expose the apparently self-assured male through the female protagonist's unexpected degree of confidence and eagerness to engage in casual sex. Reminiscent of Hayfā', the apparently naïve teenager entering an arranged marriage, story 9 in *Taksīr Rukab*, for example, unmasks the supposed sexual prowess of the male and his assumption of the female's submissiveness and physical inferiority, as well as her lack of sexual desire. The female protagonist's confidence with her sexuality subverts rape and forced sexual intercourse by men on women, representing casual sex as a desirable activity in which the female protagonist appears more versed than the rapist whom she confronts with a series of unexpected questions: 'Are you going to rape me here, in this orchard?' 'Or will you take me to your house with a bed? Are you going to rape me standing up, leaning against a tree, or lying on the grass? Will you alone rape me, or are you going to share me with your friends?'[17]

Sex and marriage in *al-Ḥiṣrim and Taksīr Rukab*: As women rise, men fall

In *al-Ḥiṣrim* the family becomes once again the object of a fierce satirical critique through the deconstruction of the relationship between husbands and wives, mothers and daughters, brothers and sisters, which stresses the female's need to satisfy her sexual appetite. Marital relations are exposed as the battleground for the conflict between the sexes. In 'al-Ṭāliq' (The divorced) the female's assertion of irresistible urgency becomes a detriment to the unexpected male victims. A widow visiting her husband's grave wilfully engages in a spontaneous sexual encounter with an unspecified man, leaving her deceased partner devoid of any agency and unable to pose a threat to her sexual drive.

> Her husband was furious, and urged her to resist until her last breath. He reminded her that respectable women would rather prefer to be slaughtered

> like ewes than surrender. Her answer came in the form of those familiar pants he had heard frequently in his bedroom. She couldn't hear him, as he announced to her in a contemptuous voice that he divorced her.[18]

This cynical attitude the widowed wife puts forward disregarding her deceased husband's cries characterizes a series of stories from *al-Ḥiṣrim* and *Taksīr Rukab* that, through sexuality, deconstructs taboos, like incest, and revered figures, such as dead husbands and religious authorities. Notably, this happens at the hands of women, who manipulate male characters and strip them of their centrality, leaving them helpless and incapable of decision-making, control and intercourse, overwhelmed by the confident and canny defiance women display.

Story 36 from *Taksīr Rukab* offers an example of how sexuality serves to expose the ineptness of male authority inside the household. The sixty-year-old protagonist Mukhtār is a bachelor with several unsuccessful and childless marriages behind him due to his sexual idleness, which the narrator describes as 'an extreme weakness that made him very forgetful and unable to save himself from embarrassing situations, unsuitable to his position in society'.[19] Yet, he falls in love with young Rashā and obtains her family's approval to marry her 'for his wealth was beyond measure'.[20] The story exposes the hypocrisy of the patriarchal family, whose approval of the marriage is guided more by their greed for wealth and prestige than by a desire to protect the female members of the family. The impotence of the protagonist suddenly seems to disappear when Rashā gets pregnant, yet every time she gives birth the children bear a striking resemblance to one of their male neighbours, which suggests that it was not Mukhtār who impregnated her. The juxtaposition between the two levels, the internal level of the story in its apparent absurdity and the external one, related to the language of power and the cornerstones of patriarchal society, can be inferred in the choice of words. The word *mukhtār*, apart from being a common (though old-fashioned) given name, is a term employed in the Arab East to refer to village chiefs and mayors, male figures of responsibility who enjoy the respect of their peers. While the confident assertion of their sexuality is the means through which female protagonists embody an anti-patriarchal stance, male impotence and incapacity becomes a means to expose the hypocrisy behind concepts such as virility, honour, mutual respect and family that nationalist authoritarian discourse in Syria has employed extensively.[21] Yet, drawing on Max Weiss's analysis of the effects of gradual liberalization of Syrian society in the early 2000s, it is difficult in this case to say who in this story has 'the last laugh'.[22] It is almost as if society as represented in the story works in circles, while leaving untouched the privileges of Mukhtār's family. In contrast the accessory and bodily dimension attached to the female protagonist is represented as the object through which ordinary male characters take their 'revenge' on the wealthy *Mukhtār.*

More than a simple satire of authoritarianism and patriarchy these stories reveal a tendency to instrumentalize female sexuality to express the degradation of the male character. In Story 22, from *Taksīr Rukab*, the wife's overwhelming verbal agency and active resourcefulness gradually overshadow the male protagonist's naivety and inaction: The protagonists Abdel Sattar ('Abd al-Sattār) and Layla have just got married when the former is put under temporary arrest for no apparent reason and ends up spending several years in jail. When Abdel Sattar is released, the whole neighbourhood is awaiting him outside prison along with his wife Layla, who looks younger than her age, as if she had grown more beautiful during his imprisonment. More relevantly though, Layla is surrounded by a group of five children who vary distinctly in their appearance, producing great embarrassment in Abdel Sattar who, nevertheless, tries to maintain a veneer of respectability in front of the community by saying, 'Legally she's my wife. Have you forgotten that I married her according to the laws of God and His Prophet?'[23] Once the social embarrassment has been dealt with, Abdel Sattar confronts Layla inside the household, asking her to identify the unfamiliar children. Layla replies defiantly, not attempting to deny her marital misconduct, pointing to the kids' resemblance to different male neighbours, a clear indication of her sustained sexual activity with members of the same community that cheerfully welcomed him back from jail.

> Abdel Sattar's fingers let go of the coffee cup, which fell to the ground and shattered, and he squatted against a wall made of rough black stone. He wanted to cry, as he had cried when beaten severely in prison, but his eyes remained dry.[24]

This story exemplifies the way in which this collection brings together the sexual and the political, the individual and the collective, confirming their inextricability as well as the undiminished political significance of Tamir's works. Linking sexual deprivation to arbitrary arrest, the authoritarian state is exposed as an emasculating force, as well as a destructive element that strips men of the role that has traditionally been assigned to them. The woman's prominence and apparent superiority, however, signals a sexualisaization of the female protagonist, and her exclusively bodily dimension. The parallel between the humiliation experienced in prison by the protagonist and the embarrassment he feels when he finds out that his neighbours slept with his wife while he was in prison bring back an element of objectification of the female body as the repository of (male) honour and respectability. These stories expose the disparity between two different and interconnected aspects in the representations of male and female protagonists that the stories of this period put forward: the greater degree of sexual agency that women have gained, acted out through the overt expression of their sexual desire and even licentiousness and the subsequent collapse of the male, overwhelmed and overshadowed by the lustful female, unable of impregnating his wife, seemingly unaware of being the object of ridicule. This confirms an idea of gender roles as mutually informed, yet the active role women play is not necessarily charged with positive connotations, and a disappointed, scornful look is shed on the changing nature of men and women. The manipulative role women play results usually in the man renouncing his masculinity and surrendering to the demands of the female.

These stories are also notable for the evident stress on the correlation, almost a cause-effect one, between the social fragmentation and the diminished masculinity of male protagonists, ascribing the greater agency of the females to a crisis of values. In addition to her anti-patriarchal taboo-breaking potential, the assertive female protagonist also reflects a sense of helplessness in the male. In this vein, Tamir's trajectory can be interpreted as an example of the disenchantment of an entire generation of politically committed Syrian authors, and his latest stories as an indication of a pessimistic glance at a society that has lost its humanity and has given up on its ambitions of freedom and emancipation.[25] Stylistically, this pessimism is expressed through a colder and seemingly indifferent language, devoid of the poetic connotations of the early period. An equally matter-of-fact style characterizes both men and women, replacing the strong contrast produced by the evocative representations of the female body. This new space and greater relevance that women take on is often symbolized by the use of sexuality as a 'weapon' that they can hold against their men, threatening to destroy their honour and their reputation.

While in the early stories women intervened occasionally as accessories of the male protagonist's struggles against a hostile environment, and as symbols of the male's quest for love, in these collections the presence of sassy female protagonists serves to reinforce the incapacity of the male to respond to the expectations of a traditional model of masculinity.

The undeniable taboo-breaking nature of these stories does not simply question a system of values; instead, it also serves as an aesthetic device that outrages the reader to lament the undermined role of men. The overtly provocative language does not entail the detailed portrayal of sexual intercourse, but rather frequently represents a weak and impotent type of masculinity that fails to meet sexual expectations embodying defeat and incapacity. If masculinity is traditionally defined by traits such as sexual prowess, courage, independence and assertiveness, the emergence of a new confident feminine voice has led to a collapse of the male, often represented as helpless, impotent and incapable of performing the sexual act.

Sex and politics in *Taksīr Rukab*: The sexualization of the female

The political implications of this new approach to female sexuality become clearer in story 49 from *Taksīr Rukab*. The setting is that of two neighbouring quarters – the inner quarter and the outer quarter – historically at odds with each other, suddenly at war again because of rumours spreading around that undermine the men's masculinity and honour. The content of the rumours involves the supposed incapacity of the men to prevent their women from sleeping with other men. Conflict seems once again imminent, until women from both quarters decide to meet secretly to find a solution and agree to put an end to the hostilities. Upon returning home to their husbands, they convince them, by having sex with them, of the pettiness of their misunderstanding with the men of the other quarter.

> They went back to their homes and tried to convince their men by night that the conflict between the two neighborhoods was nothing more than a simple misunderstanding which could happen even among brothers. Their success was dazzling, for in a few months some of their bellies started to grow. [26]

New rumours then started spreading describing the women of both quarters as submissive and acquiescent, making peace return to reign between the two quarters. At this point, the story suddenly acquires an international dimension as the secretary general of the United Nations pays a visit to the two quarters to extol the virtues of their people, and their capacity to solve conflicts. The event brings great pride to the two quarters, and after signing a peace agreement under the aegis of the United Nations harmony grows 'until they became almost one neighbor'.[27] In the end, however, what were merely rumours turn into reality with men beating their wives and cheating on them with women from other quarters.

This story makes references to the social fabric of Syria, satirizing the widespread narrative of a country populated by a mosaic of cultures and ethnicities that have coexisted relatively peacefully, despite the differences and the disparities. In comparison with the social realism of the early works, the unedifying character of these stories comes across as disengaged and politically irrelevant in the context of authoritarianism. Yet, new representations of female characters, and in particular of female sexuality, show the greater political potential of the challenge to patriarchy that the new female voice puts forward. It overturns sex as a form of *fitna* and ironically reinvents it instead as a potential solution for conflict and a source of peace.

This finds an interesting parallel in Nadine Labaki's 2011 film *Et Maintenant On Vas Ou? – Wa Halla' La-wayn?* (Where do we go now?) in the way it satirizes the narrative of peaceful coexistence between different communities in Lebanon.[28] Labaki's film is set during the Lebanese civil war in a nameless, isolated Lebanese mountain village that has witnessed on-and-off inter-sectarian warfare and periods of harmony. In the unnamed village a mosque and a church stand side by side, the imam and the priest are friends, and the Muslim and Christian cemeteries are located next to each other. The film presents a national allegory, with the village as a microcosm of Lebanese society. The notable parallels with Tamir's story emerge when the women of the village manipulate the men to prevent the echoes of the ongoing civil war from reaching them. As sectarian strife gradually starts affecting the village and its surrounding area, the women gather to conspire and concoct ways to keep their men from killing each other: first they hire a group of Ukrainian strip dancers to entertain them, then when a local Muslim boy is killed in a nearby Christian village the women drug the men by adding narcotics to their pastries, and proceed to dispose of their men's weapons. The following day, as they recover from intoxication, Muslim men wake up to find out that their wives have removed all signs of their affiliation to Islam, while Christian women have adopted the Muslim ḥijāb (headscarf). The entire village population participate in the young boy's funeral and the final scene sees men from both communities turn to their women asking for direction, unsure as to where they should bury the boy.

Similar to Labaki's film, Tamir's story pursues a vaguely idealizing approach to women as the repository of common sense in a male-dominated environment inevitably poisoned by communal strife. The similarities and parallels with Aristophanes's *Lysistrata*, in which the female population of Athens plots to end the Peloponnesian war by denying sex to the men, are obvious. Female power in the fifth-century BC Greek comedy is temporarily achieved through sexual blackmail, which ultimately succeeds in forcing men to stop the hostility. However, story 49 and other stories in this collection, similar to Labaki's film and Aristophanes's comedy, project the image of female power as manipulative, and of the female body as the only mechanism through which women manage to disrupt an unchanging environment dominated by men. While female characters have undoubtedly achieved a greater presence and express their libido more overtly, male characters retain the privilege of operating in multiple contexts and situations that transcend the merely physical dimension. Stories that address women's issues beyond the body see female characters relegated to the margins of the narration, similarly to Tamir's early stories. Challenging and satirizing an idealized model of manliness, this style still offers a greater variety of roles to male characters, while limiting the female's agency to the bodily dimension. With a few exceptions, the new female and the sexual connotations attached to female protagonists not only are unable to cancel this disparity but they also eventually limit the female's scope of action and her political agency to the sexual.

The sexualization of the female and the representation of the female body as an allegory for the nation returns in 'Imra'a jamīla' (A beautiful woman), a story from *al-Ḥiṣrim* exhibiting the same contradictions detected in the early representations of sexual abuse, which can be interpreted as an allegory for the moral decay that the author claims to detect in the country, or perhaps just the city of Damascus. As Tamir publicly acknowledged in a talk he delivered in Damascus in 2008 this story is based on many anecdotes he had heard about his native city in recent years before the collection was released.[29] Here the sexual dimension central to the allegory and the rape of 'the beautiful woman' of the title confirms the duality of a narration that, while denouncing and satirizing sexism to bring female sexual desire to the fore, remains entangled in a fundamentally polarized view on gender roles. Lumping together the nation (or perhaps the city) and the female body in order to expose corruption and fragmentation affecting a community this style perpetuates the objectification of women.

The desire to articulate the tight relationship between the sexual and the political, as well as the contradictions of the exclusively sexual and bodily role assigned to female characters, becomes manifest in another story from *Taksīr Rukab* in which the female protagonist Iqbal al-Tabbakh (Iqbāl al-Ṭabbākh) engages overtly in political activism to become a member of parliament. Again, the protagonists' political success comes as a consequence of her manipulation of men through the alluring prospect of sexual intercourse, making the most of her body as the ultimate weapon to obtain political recognition. Initially, the narrator introduces Iqbal as outraged at her husband's affair with their unattractive housemaid. Suddenly, the story takes a political turn when Iqbal decides to run for parliament, immediately enjoying the enthusiastic support of women who see her as their representative against the oppression of men. Male support, on the other hand, is only won through her irresistible sexual skills which the narrator describes through allusions and metaphors.[30]

Together with the two neighbourhoods' story quoted earlier, this story also exemplifies a style that in this collection in particular, addresses female sexuality openly and articulates a vision of equality between the sexes through the assertion of female sexual desire to the detriment of the male's privileges. However, the ever-present sexual trope reinforces an objectification of the female body which is ultimately patriarchal rather than empowering. Female characters accomplish their social and political dimension inside and outside the household exclusively through their bodies, but remain intellectually passive and insignificant, failing to truly penetrate the spaces assigned to men. What is more, Tamir's conceptualization of female power appears all the more objectifying because of the constant reference to female sexuality which, from being taboo and a subject the writer timidly hinted at in his early works, has become the sole element through which female protagonists articulate their subjectivity.

Conclusions

In the chronological analysis of Tamir's oeuvre, female sexual identity is amongst the tropes that have witnessed the most significant transformations in his latest collections. This chapter draws on the relationship between ideological fragmentation and the emergence of a new female-oriented writing in Arabic literature to show how the representations of women and female sexuality in Tamir's latest period of his career signify the maturation of the female characters through a daring assertion of their sexual desire as a stringent necessity. In the 1960s and the 1970s Tamir's protagonists' encounters with sex were introspective and self-centred, expressing great frustration and frequently denouncing the lack of contact between young boys and girls, due most often to social norms. The realistic approach that characterizes the early stories exposes a reality of oppression and sexism, backwardness and cruelty in the face of which women are helpless and are unable to counteract. The more recent stories put women at centre stage to ridicule men's inadequacy and their claims of superiority and leadership by means of a more relaxed, humorous and satirical approach to sex. The role female characters play in the stories gradually progresses from claims, complaints and demands for their recognition as possessor of sexual desires to assertion, reaffirmation and crystallization of transgressive female sexual identities that liberate their instincts, all of which represents a decisive object-subject reversal.

This style emerges in the context of fragmentation, the collapse of the totalizing ideologies and the rise of Islamism, but it also represents the accomplishment of a process of self-realization of the female protagonist that is commonly solely ascribed to female writers.[31] However, the abandonment of ideology does not deprive the text of its political significance, and clarifies the potential of the aesthetic strategies through which representations of female sexuality have developed, evolved and matured significantly throughout this author's career, as well as the ways in which it relates to the persistence of authoritarianism.

Nonetheless, the aspiration to unsettle the reader with taboo-breaking representations of women asserting their sexual desire that the stories project puts excessive emphasis on the female body, and its potentially empowering nature eventually confines the female character to the domain of the sexual, the bodily and the libidinous. Thus, the stories fail to grant female characters intellectual capacity, a precondition to truly subvert the centrality of the male in the patriarchal system. This fragmentation and multiplication of voices has entailed a new objectification of the female body; however, this focus on the body and its objectification also appears in the writings of female authors and cannot be ascribed exclusively to male writers such as Tamir.[32] The desire to give voice and centrality to the female point of view, perhaps in response to a renewed surge of more traditionally Islamic mores, seems to have to be inevitably charged with sexual connotations, partially depriving the text of its empowering potential in a patriarchal context. In other words, the process of self-realization that invests the female with significance and ideally enhances her status to that of subject is evidently undermined by the objectification that results from the recurrence of female protagonists exploiting their sexuality as a 'weapon' to gain the upper hand in their relationships with men.

5

The fall of the strong man

Virility, homosexuality and the *qabaday*

As the previous chapters have illustrated, in Tamir's trajectory the fashion of bringing together gender roles and the gendered nature of patriarchal authoritarianism has evolved in relation to historical and political transformations. The sense of inadequacy that defeat and fragmentation have produced in male protagonists and the subaltern position to which authoritarianism relegates them present us with the opportunity to discuss the aesthetic strategies through which masculinities are reinvented to address these transformations.

This chapter looks more closely at masculinity in the stories published during Tamir's self-imposed exile, in particular at themes such as homosexuality, nationalism and patriarchy, exploring male protagonists as victims of the emasculating forces of authoritarianism and patronage. Despite the supposedly diminished ideological charge that the collapse of consensus has brought about, the study of changed representations of male characters elucidates the political significance of Tamir's short stories vis-à-vis a persistent authoritarian regime. To clarify their relevance, it is necessary to situate these aesthetic developments in the context of nationalism and patriarchy, cornerstones of Syrian authoritarianism containing a normative gendered and sexual dimension. Together with the decline of nationalist, socialist and emancipatory ideologies, the consolidation of authoritarian and patriarchal regimes across the Arab East during the 1980s/1990s normalized practices that put men in a feminine position in relation to the authoritarian state. This allows us into an area of interpretation that deciphers this new and somehow crippled male that has emerged in the context of fragmentation and defeat as an attack against the symbology of power in Syria, and with a disillusioned outlook on the deterioration of said male. The analysis explores the evolution from the male-centred narrative that typified Tamir's early period to the decline of an old, strong and all-dominant type of masculinity. The presence of homosexual characters is also crucial to the political implications of masculinities and their evolution. In this vein, the analysis looks at how the mutually informed representations of femininity and masculinity in the stories under scrutiny express compliance with, and/or subversion of, a patriarchal worldview.[1]

Weak, helpless and submissive: The decline of *tough* masculinity

In addition to the greater degree of subjectivity that female characters attain, the collapse of the male protagonist's supremacy in this period comes frequently as the consequence of an internalized sense of submissiveness. While in the realm of women and female sexuality the subject/object reversal has engendered a process of empowerment through the assertion of the female sexual drive, in the case of male characters the stories of the later period exhibit a different, contradictory development. In the confrontation between citizens and the authoritarian state, works published in the early 1960s and 1970s successfully exposed the overpowering role of the representatives of the state in crushing the helpless male citizen. This male citizen – perfectly exemplified by Abū Ḥasan, the protagonist of 'Fī layla min al-layālī' – was highly aware of his own integrity and manliness. This aspect contributed to heighten the significance of the state's emasculating practices and their effects not only on a single individual but also on an ideal of man.

Although the themes of arbitrary arrest and violence at the hands of the state's representatives remain present in the later period, the idealized manliness of characters like Abū Ḥasan serves as a useful aspect of comparison to trace the transformations in the representations of male characters. The lengthy description of the protagonist's manly self-image and confidence in his own integrity accentuated the contrast between a positive model of traditional masculinity and the castrating force of the capricious authoritarian state. In turn, in the later stories the oppressor/victim relationship is transformed as the male appears as complicit in the brutal practices of the state, a victim of both the emasculating state and his self-emasculating personality. This reveals the author's acute awareness of the dynamics and strategies of domination of the Assad regime. As Lisa Wedeen has shown, the role complicity and outward obedience play in reinforcing the power of the authoritarian state makes everyone complicit in the self-enforcing strategies of domination. This deconstructs the state versus citizens binary, attributing an equal amount of responsibility to the state's practices of coercion and the citizens' continued, albeit hypocritical, acceptance.[2]

For an example of this new obedient male, Farīd al-Murabbaʿ, the protagonist of story 58 from *Taksīr Rukab* extols his easily 'bribable' personality in front of the interrogators when the police arrest him in the early hours of the morning with a preposterous accusation: he refuses to take bribes. He proudly asserts his descent from a family in which no one would ever refuse 'the blessing of a bribe'.[3] After beating and torturing Farīd for days for denying the accusation levelled against him, the interrogator agrees to release him, accepting Farīd's offer of a monthly bribe and the prospect of increasing its amount every month.

In addition to the male protagonist's own self-image and internalized submissiveness, the collapse of the male's supremacy in this period comes frequently as the consequence of the greater degree of subjectivity that female characters attain, testimony to the mutually informing relationship between femininities and masculinities. In *Sa-naḍḥak*, the male protagonists often project a model of weak, unreliable masculinity, and gender roles become a tool to exemplify decay. For example, Muṣṭafā al-Amīr, the protagonist of 'al-Mutanakkir' (The disguised) camouflages himself as an eight-year-old when his fiancée Kawthar visits him to announce her pregnancy to him. Belittling and infantilizing himself in order to avoid his responsibilities, Muṣṭafā al-Amīr appears to Kawthar as a child, signalling the emergence of a cowardly male who, faced with the prospect of fatherhood, fails to meet the expectations of masculinity.[4]

The degradation of masculinity in story 47 in *Taksīr Rukab* is rendered through the gradual fragmentation of the male protagonist Said (Saʿīd) and the removal of his moustache in an effort to please a woman. As the Lebanese novelist Hasan Daoud notes, in the Arab tradition (*turāth*), preserved in popular sayings and folk takes, the moustache stands for masculinity and respectability, as well as a form of symbolic currency employed in honour disputes. The thicker it is, the stronger the display of manhood it reinforces.[5]

Said, however, does not hesitate to shave it off to please his nameless beautiful and daring mistress. The consequences are inevitable, and as Said looks at himself in the mirror he realizes he does not recognize his own reflection. The removal of the moustache, the symbol of his masculinity, introduces a process of gradual emasculation of the protagonist that amounts to humiliation.

> He then looked into the mirror and saw there a man he did not recognize. 'Who are you?' he asked.
>
> - 'My name is Raghid', said the man with the shaved mustache.
>
> Raghid then laughed a merry and mocking laughter and said to Said, 'the moment you shaved your mustache you disappeared. You didn't exist any more'.
>
> - 'Don't gloat or feel glad', said Said to Raghid. 'In a few days my hair will grow back the way it was because it's very thick and has always giver barbers a hard time'.[6]

Men's incapacity to stand up to women's demands results in their ideal as well as physical fragmentation and loss of identity. The competition that the attractive female protagonist induces in the male characters pushes them to symbolically castrate themselves, first by shaving off their moustaches, then their hair. Even Said's reflection splits up and sees himself reflected in the mirror as yet a different man who introduces himself as Walīd. An argument ensues between the three contradicting personalities of the protagonist, exposing a process through which the male becomes incapable of pleasing the female. 'I'm married to the beautiful and intelligent Amal who's impossible to please', argues Walīd; 'she only loves my mustache and considers it a sign of true manhood';[7] 'She used to pass her hand through my hair and say it was the hair of a black stallion'.[8] But upon finding out what Said has done, Amal asks him for an explanation, to which he replies first by making up that he has cancer. Contradicted by his two reflections in the mirror, he then claims to have been summoned to join the army. When Amal asks him to compensate her for the shock caused by his lies, the protagonist embraces her and they engage in sexual intercourse, which the narrator describes as paying 'whatever compensation he owed'.[9] The woman's apparent superiority again reinforces her sexualization, and her exclusively bodily dimension, as a means to visualize the fragmentation of the male-dominated society. Such transgressive imagery in Tamir's later stories does not promote a liberation of sexual mores and free relations between men and women but rather decries a diminished role for men in the public sphere, in line with similar trends detected elsewhere in contemporary Arabic literature.[10]

The satire of delusional masculinity: The *qabaḍay*

Al-Ḥiṣrim is a collection characterized by the incommunicability between generations and the widespread disadvantages brought about by patriarchy in its various embodiments. The title *al-Ḥiṣrim* (Arabic for sour grapes) borrows from the biblical tradition, hinting at a well-known Arab proverb that goes: 'The fathers eat sour grapes and their children's tongue gets bitter.'[11] The proverb is usually interpreted as a metaphor for the negative effects that the mistakes parents make have on their children, an allegory for the price younger generations have to pay for their predecessors' bad choices.[12] The title of this collection suggests the intergenerational motif that characterizes most stories, with particular consideration to the consequences of past and current habits and practices on the future generations.

In addition, the title also alludes to Aesop's famous 'the fox and the grapes' story, comparing the sourness of the grapes the fox leaves behind to the bitterness of life in the *al-Qawīq* quarter,[13] imagined perhaps as a microcosm for Syria. The word *ḥiṣrim* itself connotes sourness and crudeness, describing something that is half-grown and immature, a metaphor for a world that possesses the seed of change and emancipation but is still unprepared for the imaginary harvest. The metaphorical bitterness that children inherit from their fathers refers to a set of social habits and behaviours, a corrupt mentality passed on from one generation to the next, that usually originates in the home and from the mistrust between members of the same family.

In addition, the original reinvention of historical figures, widespread in contemporary Arabic literature and, according to some, a trait of Arabic literary postmodernism,[14] typifies most of Tamir's later collections including *al-Ḥiṣrim*. Alongside the active role female characters play in shaping the male's identity and manipulating him for their own benefit, symbols charged with cultural and historical connotations intervene to reinforce the contrast with an ideal masculinity that male protagonists are seldom able to live up to. Moreover, the biblical proverb and the relationship between fathers and sons are far from being the only cultural reference. In fact, this collection opens with a quote from the Qur'ān, surah Yūsuf, almost as if to warn the imagined reader against family members as the primary actors of betrayal and distrust.

> {My son, tell your brothers nothing of this dream or they may plot to harm you.}[15]

Most of *al-Ḥiṣrim*'s stories are set in the microcosm of the popular al-Qawīq quarter where the protagonists experience dependency and patronage in circumstances told in a style charged with Arabic cultural connotations. Khiḍr ʿAllūn, the protagonist in ʿal-Muhārasha' (The quarrel)[16] and ʿMaṣraʿ khanjar' (Death of a dagger),[17] is an example of the original variety of roles performed by male protagonists, as well as of the historical and mythical symbols of masculinity that Tamir incorporates in the stories of this collection. ʿAl-Muhārasha' and ʿMaṣraʿ khanjar' could be seen as two parts of the same story, revolving around a quarrel between Khiḍr and Umm ʿAlī,[18] stirred by Najīb Bey al-Baqqār, the richest man in the quarter, who manipulates the opponents for his own benefit, exploiting the former's pride and vanity and the latter's haughtiness and poverty. The narrator introduces *al-Qawīq* as 'notorious for its wealthy, who would kill their mothers if that had granted them more money' as well as 'for its rude men, who would never say no to a bloody wrangle and would happily go to prison. Men such as Khiḍr ʿAllūn, who cut his left ear in court in front of the judge and ate it with great pleasure.'[19] Without mentioning it directly, the narrator outlines the protagonist's profile as a *qabaḍay*, a colloquial term used to this day in the Syrian vernacular to describe a generous and morally upright man, but which traditionally in Ottoman Syria was a real-life figure, a manly tough guy and an instrument of the local notables to ensure their control over areas of the city. As Philip Shoukri Khoury recounts, the *qabaḍayāt* (plural for *qabaḍay*) were symbols and almost authorities of the popular (*shaʿbī*) quarters of Damascus and an expression of the city's multiple traditions and customs. They were a prominent feature of life in the city, renowned for their strength and moral righteousness, with an intimate and loyal connection to the popular quarters (*al-ḥārāt al-shaʿbiyya* in Arabic) to which the *qabaḍayāt* belonged and whose honour they defended. Far from being role models, though, they also possessed a darker side, in that they were usually violent unsophisticated instruments of power who used their physical prowess to serve the authority of the local notables, known as beys (*beyk* in Arabic). Although widely respected and revered, the *qabaḍayāt* possessed no political or financial power and were usually under the protection of beys who employed them to run their patronage networks.[20]

It is important to note how the narrator sets these two stories in contemporary times, an aspect the reader can infer from the occasional mention of cars, paved roads and plastic surgery, which did not form part of the urban landscape in Ottoman Syria. Nowadays, the delusional and romanticized *qabaḍay* model of masculinity that Khiḍr represents – far from being ideal – becomes in this case the object of ridicule in the second story (*Masra' khanjar*), eventually causing the male's own disenfranchisement and demise. The story begins with the protagonist Khiḍr 'Allūn discussing with his mother the prospect of getting married and settling down, as well as having plastic surgery to get his ear fixed. His refusal to accept his mother's advice and the model of resilient virility he projects comes across as a delusional myth modelled on the sixth-century Arab knightly poet and warrior 'Antara Ibn Shaddād,[21] as a symbol of a long-lost ideal of courage and integrity. The protagonist entertains imaginary conversations with 'Antara, who functions almost as his consciousness, instructing him on everyday issues and on how to resist the feminization of society. According to this protagonist and his imaginary friend, what makes a true *qabaḍay* these days is not his strength or his courage, but rather his ability to distinguish himself from women. The role of 'Antara's myth becomes more relevant when the emasculating forces of the modern state intervene to deprive the male protagonist of his dagger, the token of his masculinity, which underpins his subjectivity and serves as a phallic metaphor. During an ordinary stop-and-search, two police constables confiscate Khiḍr's dagger, the dearest object he owns, symbolically castrating him and leaving him dumbfounded.

> Khiḍr sat down speechless, feeling ashamed as though he was naked.
>
> - 'A man who gives up on his knife isn't a man and he only deserves to sit among women', said 'Antara Ibn Shaddād to Khiḍr.
>
> - 'But it's the police who took it', said Khiḍr.
>
> - 'As if you didn't know that they're men too', said 'Antara Ibn Shaddād, 'people like you and me who will die one day, just like you and me.'
>
> - 'Without my dagger, I'm as fragile as an old, paralysed woman', said Khiḍr.[22]

Khiḍr tries to retrieve his dagger through Najīb al-Baqqār, himself the remake of an equally important traditional Damascene figure, the Bey to whom *qabaḍayāt* were loyal and dependent. But al-Baqqār's intercession with the authorities remains unsuccessful, and to add insult to injury, Khiḍr discovers that the police sold his dagger to a foreign female tourist. Feeling weak and helpless in the story's closure he is run over and killed by a car after wandering aimlessly in an affluent area away from his quarter.

Comparing this story to Abū Ḥasan's and his working-class model of manliness again sheds light on the transformations gender roles have undergone in Tamir's oeuvre. The denunciation of inequality and class segregation have a significant presence in the later stories set in the *al-Qawīq* quarter, and the restaging of the old Damascus quarters serves to create a microcosm characterized by patronage and dependency. However, Khiḍr's estrangement is also a consequence of his own delusion, and his steadfast commitment to his knife, which ultimately serves as an instrument not of his own, but of the Bey's power. The historical figure of 'Antara and the imaginary conversations the protagonist entertains with him reinforce the contradictory nature of the protagonist's obstinacy and self-denial even after his death. The collective dimension of gender roles emerges particularly in the authority of the state, as well as of patronage and wealth that rise above masculinity, deconstructing the protagonist's ideal of honour and respectability embodied by his knife. The attempt made by Najīb al-Baqqār to intercede on behalf of Khiḍr confirms masculinity and male solidarity as a façade behind which power relations hide, revealing them as the decisive factors which determine the man's position in society. The different connotations that the context and class identity attribute to masculinity successfully expose the performative nature of gender roles, acted out in accordance with socially constructed norms and patterns that make them pertinent or not, a product of class-bound gender ideologies and an overall repressive political atmosphere.[23]

'Al-Muṭarbash' (from *ṭarbūsh*, Arabic for fez, *muṭarbash* someone who wears a fez) also revolves around a *qabaḍay*, Manṣūr al-Ḥāf, another character embodying a mythical model of masculinity. 'Manṣūr al-Ḥāf was a man from Damascus, feared and revered by the fiercest men. A man with the composure of a calm sea who would gladly go to jail as though he was going to a summer resort, and when he was discharged he would say, 'only a stupid man would be happy to move from a small jail to a big one'.[24] His loyalty to his wife Nazīha also highlights his *qabaḍayesque* gallantry, but comes to an end when she asks him to take off his fez, causing the protagonist to repudiate his wife. As the story unfolds the fez's symbolism is expanded to connote the protagonist's masculinity, as well as nationalism and resilience, and resistance against foreign occupation. The conflict between the protagonist and his wife takes an unexpected turn when the fez dispute acquires an international dimension – the moment the narrator reinvents an important moment in Syria's history. Naziha's lamentations for her husband's repudiation reached 'the ears of the French general Henri Gouraud, who set off to save her, and led his troops victoriously into Damascus, stained with the blood of the city's sons killed in Maysalūn'.[25]

The story is loosely based on historical events and the 1922 League of Nations mandate through which France claimed control of the territories of today's Syria and Lebanon.[26] General Henri Gouraud mentioned in the story was a real general who led the French troops against the Syrian nationalist resistance in the battle of Maysalūn in July 1920,[27] and was subsequently appointed France's high commissioner for Syria.[28] The importance of these events and of the twenty-six-year-long French mandate for Syria's contemporary history cannot be overstated. Particularly in both Syrian and Pan-Arab nationalism, French rule entailed a process of carving up the countries of Greater Syria, known in Arabic as Bilād al-Shām, a vast territory including today's Syria, Lebanon, Jordan and parts of Turkey and Palestine. Although Bilād al-Shām had never been a unified state, in Syria's collective memory it is considered a culturally and linguistically homogenous entity. The French proceeded to divide this whole into small sectarian-based, semi-independent entities and by the time Syria gained its independence in 1946 the territories of Bilād al-Shām had shrunk dramatically.[29]

The connection between the wife's cry for help and the subsequent French expedition reinvents the significance of the Syrian defeat in Maysalūn, using the male/female dynamics between Manṣūr and his wife to symbolize colonization at the hands of the imperial Western powers. After taking power in Damascus, General Henri Gouraud proceeds to ban the fez in the entire country, but Manṣūr refuses to remove it and is arrested. Summoned by the French authorities as the only transgressor of the fez ban, the hero's defiant resilience arouses the French general's irritation, who sentences him to decapitation, which the protagonist accepts peacefully, reciting passages from the Qur'an.[30]

The ironic twist to the heroism and resilience of the protagonist is provided by the ambiguous symbolic value of the fez, a type of headgear originally from Morocco but popularized by Sultan Mahmud II in the Ottoman Empire.[31] Simultaneously a symbol of past Ottoman identity and a fetish that embodies the protagonist's resistance to the new occupiers and a token of his masculinity, the fez's ambiguity serves to bring together core elements of Syria's collective memory. Syria had been part of the Ottoman Empire for over four centuries between 1516 and 1919 when the Syrian Arab Kingdom was established, then dissolved shortly afterwards following the battle of Maysalūn. The virility of the protagonist is again exemplified by his courage as well as by his capacity to love a woman, in contrast with the emasculating authority impersonated by the tyrannical foreign colonizers. Similar to the figure of 'Antara bin Shaddād, this protagonist equally embodies a traditional model of masculinity in decline, symbolized by society's lack of respect for the fez. At the same time, the fez and its resonance in historical terms proves a powerful literary device to satirize a model of delusional masculinity. This is not the first time Tamir satirizes a peculiarly masculine trait of stubbornness and a self-erasing attitude; this story is reminiscent of 'al-Liḥā' (The beards), published originally in April 1967. Here, the male inhabitants of an unspecified city, confronted by the prospect of annihilation at the hands of the Mongol conqueror Tamerlane, choose death before accepting to have their beards shaven.[32] A dark irony surrounds the narrator's view of the protagonist's blind and illogical acceptance of sacrifice, excluding simplistic and unequivocal interpretations.[33] In addition, the multi-layered and ambivalent style that pokes fun at elements of history and tradition while encouraging multiple viewpoints of the same story introduces elements of postmodern writing. As Ulrike Stehli-Werbeck observes, the parodistic attitude towards elements of tradition reinvents the Arab *turāth* in order to satirize a delusional worldview.[34]

Furthermore, it is important to point out the political significance of the *qabaḍay* in contemporary Syrian culture. The changing connotations the term possesses in Syrian drama series, an extremely popular and prolific genre, with perhaps much greater influence and impact than literature, testify to the relevance that these manly figures retain.[35] Analysing the transformations in the construction of the *qabaḍay* in drama series from the 1960s to the present day, Rebecca Joubin has highlighted the connection between the downfall of the manly and protective figure and the emergence of more equal gender relations.[36] Such multi-layered, evocative stories might come across at a first glance as sexist and patriarchal for the significantly more intense presence and agency male characters still enjoy. However, while intellectually sophisticated and politically charged subjectivities are interpreted exclusively by male protagonists, they are also most frequently the victims of the narrator's sarcastic remarks. While it is still the case that men retain a criticality that women achieve only through their bodily dimension, this element becomes a tool to satirize the male's supposed superiority, exposing the self-mutilating, delusional and deceptive nature of a dominant and generally accepted notion of what is male/female. Although male protagonists such as Manṣūr embody a political dimension that female protagonists do not attain, their soundness is hardly idealized and the interpretative effort that the style involves engages the reader to deconstruct the relationship between men and women.

Homosexual male desire as the sign of decay

An examination of masculinity cannot overlook the role homosexuality plays in producing it. In patriarchal systems of signification the position homosexual men occupy in the gender hierarchy of dominant and complicit masculinities remains right at the bottom, and normative homosexual traits, such as the pleasure derived from passive anal sex, join normative feminine traits to define everything that masculinity is not.[37] To this day, homosexuality and homosexual practices remain technically illegal in the Syrian penal code,[38] and addressing the subject openly is as frowned upon in Syria as anywhere else, if not more. Applying this approach to Arabic literature and society, ideal models of masculinity are frequently constructed in opposition to deviant models and in relation to presumed feminine characteristics.[39]

The sexualized and erotic aspect of Arabic literary production before the 1980s pointed to the essentially male nature of war, the liberation movement, political activism, imprisonment, and confrontation with imperialism.[40] In this vein, Arab nationalism and Arabic literature, deeply influenced by a patriarchal worldview, not only understood the concepts of manhood and womanhood as signifiers for the relationship between men and women but expanded their significance to apply them to the relationship between human beings and the world. Hence, power relations could only be conceived in terms of strict dichotomies of domination/submission, strength/weakness and, crucially, male/female.[41]

Homosexual desire, love and intercourse are practically absent from Tamir's early stories, with the exception of timid allusions to homosexuality as the direct consequence of (hetero)sexual deprivation and disenfranchisement. In Tamir's later works the subject retains negative connotations that serve to reinforce the pattern of male helplessness. In 'Ḥamlat Nabulyūn' (Napoleon's expedition), the restaging of historical events and personalities acquires a gendered dimension. The French emperor's famous expedition to Egypt is reinvented in contemporary terms, set in today's Damascus, which Napoleon occupies enjoying the submissive reception of the city's dignitaries and religious authorities. The story takes an unexpected turn to the sexual inversion of the male/female relationship between colonial powers and colonized victims: Napoleon's wife Joséphine taints the emperor's reputation by engaging in repeated sexual intercourse introducing 'the young Damascenes to what they did not know';[42] the emperor's colonizing/phallic prowess on the other hand is reversed to represent him in homosexual terms. Sad and depressed about his wife's scandals, Napoleon seeks the help of a local sheikh, who advises him to attend the local hammams, where the emperor finally finds gratification

> for being under the masseurs' bodies made him imagine his army conquering the entire world. Napoleon Bonaparte led a happy life in Damascus, but the French government sent someone to abduct him and bring him back to France where he spent the rest of his life sighing in sorrow and distress every time he recalled Damascus and its men.[43]

This reversal and the 'revenge' of the feminized East on the male colonizer confirms a conceptualization of the relationship between East and West that remains sexualized, one of strength and challenge, shaped by dichotomies such as activity/passivity and positivity/negativity. As Ṭarābīshī explains, according to this view there can never possibly be room for two males. One of the two has to prove his manhood to provide evidence of the womanhood of the other.[44]

This after all remains in line with the examples of same-sex intercourse in modern Arabic literature, which can be grouped into three main categories:

homosexual desire as an element of a bygone past and as an aspect of traditional society, frowned upon in modern times, or as a disease leading to death and suicide, or as humiliation at the hands of a foreign occupant with the colonizer performing the role of the active partner. There is no 'happy' homosexuality and this variety of representations ultimately conceptualizes same-sex relations as a lack of masculinity and deviancy.[45] The representations of male same-sex intercourse in *Taksīr Rukab* contribute to add a further category to this, that is, homosexuality as an internalized form of submissiveness to both women and authoritarianism. In Story 24, set in the imaginary village of Dhaghbit (Ẓaghbīt), same-sex intercourse is introduced through a nameless male thief who is said to have raped the village's men inside their houses. The narrator first sketches the village as dominated by men, as an environment where 'a woman could not even mutter "good morning" to her husband unless he gave her permission'. When a mysterious figure referred to as 'a strange man who wanted to rob and rape'[46] appears, the village's reaction is one of widespread silence and hypocrisy. Soon, however, a major development ensues as 'the women of Dhaghbit started to ignore their husband's orders and did exactly as they pleased'.[47] It is only when an old, retired soldier catches the 'strange man' entering his house that the truth is revealed by the thief/rapist: the men of Dhaghbit welcomed the rapist into their houses and asked him to rape them repeatedly in front of their wives. Attacking the contradictions underpinning sexist and patriarchal society, the narrator contrasts the male villagers' desire to be raped with their performance in public and their despotic relationships with their wives. Confronted with the shameful prospect of exposing his fellow villagers' honour, the old man decides to summon the men that the thief claims to have raped and seeks their advice. In the closure, the same men murder the old man and the rapist, restoring the village's order and honour. 'The women of Dhaghbit went back to listening to their husbands' orders with a shudder, rushed to obey them, and wished that Dhaghbit would vanish under the snows.'[48]

This story echoes the way Syrian and Arab cinema have addressed sexuality and masculinity using the protagonists' incapacity to fulfil their role as men to represent the frustration of defeat and helplessness. In the climax scene of Michel Khleifi's 'Wedding in Galilee' (1987) the young groom is incapable of fulfilling his family's expectations on his wedding night; the sheet upon which he sleeps with his newly married wife Sāmiya needs to be stained with her blood in order to give evidence of his virility to the members of the community. However, he is incapable of consummating the marriage and Sāmiya has to penetrate herself with her fingers in order to take her own virginity and spill the drops of blood required to protect the family's honour.[49] Relevant examples of this contrast and hypocrisy in contemporary Syrian cultural production include movies written and directed by 'Abd al-Laṭīf 'Abd al-Ḥamīd. His *Layālī Ibn Āwa* (Nights of the Jackals) associates the man's impotence with defeat and weakness. Here, the male protagonist's failure is exacerbated by the empowerment of the female. Realized under the supervision of the state-controlled National Cinema Organisation of Syria in 1988, it presents clear parallels to Tamir's motifs and images. Set in rural Syria during the years of the United Arab Republic and later of the 1967 defeat to Israel, the protagonists are members of a working-class family of peasants who struggle to make ends meet while facing the challenges of urbanization and modernization. The paterfamilias Abū Kamāl, a seemingly self-assured and confident father, suffers from sleep deprivation, scared as he is by howling jackals that can only be chased away by his wife's whistles – the same wife that he beats and humiliates during the day, yelling out his frustration at the emasculating forces of poverty and disenfranchisement. Just as the bossy father of 'Abd al-Ḥamīd's *Layālī Ibn Āwa* mistreats his wife, keeping up the appearances of a paterfamilias who commands respect and reverence from his family, although he is incapable of providing for them, the men of Dhaghbit reveal their weakness and hypocrisy when confronted with the prospect of being raped. In an environment where men belittle women, the submissiveness to authoritarianism that the former have internalized serves to overturn a patriarchal logic. In Tamir's story the critique of the male-dominated society is taken to an extreme through the homosexual trope: not only are men incapable of protecting their household but they also desire to be humiliated and subjugated.

In Story 42 from *Taksīr Rukab*, the protagonist Taha (Ṭāhā) is a man who 'enjoyed being submissive'.[50] His wife Iffat ('Iffat) easily manipulates him and vents her frustration at his sexual incapacity by kicking him out of the house, sending him to look for some entertainment or play with the kids in the street. After wandering around the city, the protagonist is stopped by a stranger, whom the narrator describes as 'a tall man with broad shoulders, protruding eyeballs, and a thick moustache', an intimidating figure who forces Taha into the basement of an unfinished building and rapes him at gunpoint. Familiarity with Syrian regime thugs, commonly referred to in the Syrian vernacular as *shabbīḥa*, may induce the reader to interpret this 'tall man' as their embodiment, but the story offers no further indication to substantiate this speculation.[51] The humiliation Taha experiences inside the household at the hands of his unsatisfied wife is paralleled by the degradation that he experiences at the hands of a thug outside in the form of sexual abuse. The relevance of the story resides not only in the portrayal of same-sex intercourse as degradation and humiliation but also, more relevantly, in the victim's ambiguous reaction to the abuse.

> Taha felt hungry and thought it was strange. He took from his pocket a piece of chocolate which the stranger had given to him, and was about to toss it to the ground in disgust. But the hand that held the chocolate lifted it to his mouth and pushed it inside, and his teeth chewed it until it was mixed with saliva. [. . .] He was surprised by his feeling of pride when the stranger said that he was handsome and delectable. He wished his wife could hear that. [52]

The diminished masculinity of the protagonist has transformed him to the extent that he has internalized obedience and submissiveness, symbolized by his inability to control his bodily movements, his hands and his arms. Even though he still grasps the humiliation of what his body has become used to do, the protagonist cannot help repeating the same humiliating gestures; the seemingly conflicting thoughts that the traumatic experience of rape elicits leave him trapped and helpless. Similarly to the structure of 'al-Numūr fī al-yawm al-'āshir', with the proud tiger gradually growing accustomed to the taste of grass provided by its trainer, little by little the individual becomes accustomed to swallowing the same chocolate that his rapist administers to him. The narrator overturns gender roles to highlight the despicable decay of masculinity, with women representing not a 'fair sex' but playing a dominant role since their men are incapable of living up their expectations. This reversal of gender roles turns men into objects unable to uphold their reputation and their honour, desiring to be raped, incapable of making decisions and of deciding of their own destiny, objects at the mercy of their women. Their incapacity to confront their women inside their home is reproduced outside by the inability to defend themselves and their dignity against the oppressing force of the emasculating state. Thus, the increasingly powerful and sexually confident role women play joins the capricious forces of the state in undermining the male.

This said, the scarce and ambiguous nature of stories about homosexual intercourse is representative of a reticence to address the topic in contemporary Arabic literature that has been defined as 'the invisible desire'.[53] While censorship certainly remains a possible explanation, it is also safe to argue that the disparity in the ways and the frequency with which Tamir brings to the stage heterosexual and homosexual desire is revealing of a moralism that advocates a form of normalized heterosexual equality between the two sexes. Same-sex intercourse appears exclusively as a means to express the decline of a strong masculinity, thus carrying negative connotations. This confirms the inclination to employ a weakened male protagonist to lament the decadence and helplessness of a traditionally strong type of manhood, instead of exploring masculinity in its multiple shades. Homosexual desire serves to portray a subdued and compliant male as the victim of his own lack of masculinity and self-respect, denouncing submissiveness to authoritarian practices rather than denouncing oppression and tyranny. The significant shift happens in the realm of sexual practices changing the focus from the emasculating forces of the authoritarian state to the self-emasculating nature of the subdued and delusional male.

Conclusions

This chapter has analysed the representations of male protagonists in Tamir's recent works in the context of a split between literature and nationalist ideology, and in relation to the persistence of neopatriarchal authoritarianism. Highlighting the pervasive role of female characters reveals a lasting tendency to instrumentalize the female body and her sexual agency to symbolize the demise of the male at the hands of the authoritarian state. Particularly in stories about arbitrary arrest and the volatile nature of power, politics is reconfirmed as essentially male. This inclination has been analysed extensively by Ṭarābīshī, who has significantly drawn attention to subtexts that emphasize the phallic nature of political activism in works authored by both male and female writers across the Arab world. However, while Ṭarābīshī explains this phenomenon in relation to the patriarchal ideology of a backwards society,[54] the persistence of a male-centred view on society in Tamir's later works reflects a sense of pessimism at the persistence of authoritarianism and its normalization.

Gender roles retain a decisive function in the stories under study in this chapter, through stories that put forward a vulnerable, subordinate and weak model of masculinity. Looking at gender configurations as mutually informed, instead of separate universes with disparate political significance, this chapter has elucidated how the collapse of the male protagonist's supremacy emerges as the consequence of the greater degree of female agency, as well as of the man's own self-image. However, while the social and political dimension of the female comes to the fore only through her sexuality, the disintegration of the male embodies a larger variety of articulations. The analysis of a variety of symbols employed to signify masculinity and the feminization of the male characters, in contrast with the exclusively sexual dimension of the female protagonists, has also served to show the greater relevance that male characters still retain. This hardly amounts to male supremacism, and the stylistic devices of irony and historical restaging serve to expose a dominant and virile type of masculinity as delusional. Tamir transforms sex and gender relations into a suggestive means to denounce oppression, stagnation and political hypocrisy, depicting male protagonists characterized by sexual incapacity as well as by a form of homosexual desire that comes across as a perversion to expose the decay of the individual's masculinity.

This analysis has also shown how, although a new female subjectivity has emerged in the works of the later period, exemplified by the stories addressed in the previous chapter, the exclusively bodily and sexual role that these new female protagonists perform leaves male protagonists with the advantage of embodying multi-dimensional subjectivities, as opposed to the one-dimensional sexual female. Examples from *al-Ḥiṣrim* and *Taksīr Rukab* have shown how, in addition to the bodily and the libidinous elements of the male's personality, the male's disintegration and loss of subjectivity is also articulated through the intellectual and the political, often through a direct confrontation with the authoritarian state and its oppressive practices. In other words, although the stories analysed elsewhere demonstrate a significant degree of maturation in the greater variety of roles assigned to women, this chapter has shown how the language inevitably reveals a conceptualization of men and women in society performing two strict, separate and polarized subjectivities. The greater variety of roles that male protagonists perform, in Syrian and Arabic literature traditionally, as well as in Tamir's works more specifically, suggests a broader range of interpretations and greater political significance. Similar to the explicit sexual passages constructed around female protagonists, the representations of male sexuality also witness a transformation towards the provocative and the transgressive.

Conclusion

This study has analysed Zakariyya Tamir's short stories and artistic trajectory, in particular the transformations in the representations of male and female characters in his stories. The five chapters have shown how no clear-cut definition of Tamir's short stories as unquestionably sexist, or feminist, or patriarchal is acceptable. The analysis has instead clarified the inextricable relationship between the works of this writer and the historical conditions in which they appeared, as well as the centrality that familial relations, sexuality, marriage and gender roles have retained in his short stories.

Looking at Tamir's very early stories in comparison with the literary trends popular in Syria and elsewhere, while examining the formal peculiarities of his works, has reaffirmed the avant-garde aesthetics his stories contributed to introduce in the Arabic short story at the time of his beginnings as a writer. Situating Tamir's trajectory in the context of different conceptualizations of literary commitment popular in Syria and the Arab East in the decades between the 1950s and late 1970s has shown the peculiarly autonomous idea of commitment to which the author subscribed as being intimately linked with a complex engagement with aesthetics. A close analysis of the language has also clarified the male-centred character of a style which was organic to the struggles for modernity, national emancipation and against class inequality and authoritarianism as performed almost exclusively by male protagonists. This is exemplified in Tamir's very early stories by the greater frequency of male protagonists, as well as by the objectification of female characters, who usually remain marginal and serve as accessories of the male individual's aspirations. The male's quest for material stability, freedom and love underpins a vast number of stories in which female characters appear as the object of the protagonist's lust and desires for love, sexual intercourse and stability. Aesthetically, this is reflected by a disparity in the registers employed to represent male and female characters, and by the dissimilar metaphors the narrator resorts to in order to convey the descriptions of the protagonists according to their gender. While the internal dimension of the male protagonist is what concerns the narrator the most, not his physical appearance, the lengthy and evocative illustrations of the female body and beauty reinforce a polarization of male and female subjectivity. The introduction by Tamir of the stream of consciousness in his stories – a most significant innovation charged with great political implications at the time his early stories appeared – takes the reader into the male protagonists' minds, voicing their inner feelings, travelling back and forth in time to explore past experiences and their effects on their present situation. The opposite, that is, the female character clearly articulating their desire for love and sex, emerges considerably less frequently only in a handful of examples, which nevertheless possess great significance in the historical development of the themes of sexuality and gender roles. These relevant, albeit infrequent, examples of aesthetically evocative and highly poetic stories that Tamir published in the early 1960s have shown an acute awareness of sexual drives in women as deeply embedded in the author's existentialist and anti-patriarchal stance. In addition, the capacity of this author to articulate representations of female desire contradicts the idea of this theme as a prerogative of female writers.

The existentialist exploration of the male individual's inner universe and the evocative representations of female protagonists, putting forward a genuinely female point of view on female sexual desire in a patriarchal context, gave place to a greater focus on the increasingly pervasive presence of the authoritarian state in the life of citizens in the period 1970–8. The analysis of this theme has revealed the stories' capacity to capture the gendered dimension of authoritarian practices of arbitrary arrest and torture, as well as the contradictions in the disparity between the representations of male characters as emasculated victims of tyranny on the one hand and of female characters as the accessory repository of the man's humiliation on the other. Particularly in stories in which the practices of arbitrary arrest, torture and humiliation are addressed more explicitly, only the male protagonists appear charged with agency vis-à-vis power. In other words, while the significance of transgressive portrayals of female characters and the daring acknowledgement of sex as enjoyable is undeniable, stories that signal an increased concern with the detrimental impact of authoritarian practices leave female characters at the margins. The political arena and the confrontation between citizens and despotism in these stories remained a men's issue.

Drawing on Connell's conceptualization of *dominant* and *complicit* masculinity has helped ascertain how, while overall Tamir's stories never put forward an openly male-supremacist view, the greater degree of agency that male characters enjoy revealed a fundamentally male conceptualization of modernism as well as of the quest for freedom in his early stories. This tendency allows an interpretation of gender roles in Tamir's early works that is fundamentally *complicit* to a patriarchal worldview, at the same time denouncing the belittling attitude of patriarchal tradition towards women in various stories, exposing the misogyny of both men and women in others, expressing occasionally, albeit relevantly, open acknowledgement of the female's necessity for sexual intercourse, but essentially revealing all these aspects as secondary in the broader quest for emancipation. Ultimately the analysis of gender roles and patriarchy in Tamir's oeuvre has clarified the political significance of a style that was organic to the project of national liberation, state building and modernization to which, however, the issue of gender equality had represented a subordinate aspect.

The intimate relationship that cultural production in the Arab world entertained with the grand narratives of national liberation and modernism until the 1970s, and that was subsequently put into question by the experience of war defeat and political fragmentation, has helped to situate the developments in Tamir's stories from the 1970s onwards. The signs of a distancing from the *ḥadāthī* worldview materialize in Tamir's early period, and come to the fore in a group of four collections the author published between 1994 and 2002 from his self-imposed expatriation to London and Oxford. Aesthetically, this later period presents the crystallization of compilations of short stories that revolve around a set of subjects as opposed to the early collections which brought together stories published at different times in local magazines and were characterized by greater thematic variety. This increased thematic homogeneity stands in sharp contrast with the stylistic fragmentation of the text, especially in the first two collections from this period, *Nidā' Nūḥ* and *Sa-naḍḥak*, which feature the extensive presence of multiple-part, segmented short stories. Thematically, this fragmentation is reflected first by a sense of pessimism permeating the language, signalling the decline of the modernist and nationalist causes of emancipation to which Tamir's early works – albeit in an original way – were organic. The narration exhibits a more nuanced and multifarious approach to the bodily and sexual dimension of the stories that can be labelled as postmodern, which nevertheless does not amount to indifference and a clear-cut separation from social and political developments in Syria and the Arab East. In this process of departure and distancing from *éngagé* and ideological aspects, the stories have retained a significant political charge, particularly in the representations of sexuality and desire.

The analysis has highlighted the increased presence of assertive female characters confidently expressing their sexuality not in response to patriarchal tradition, but actively shaping the masculinity of male protagonists. A more equal approach to gender roles, especially in the confrontation between authoritarianism and ordinary citizens, a richer and more diverse approach to masculinity and the mutually informed understanding of gender roles has emerged, crystallized more manifestly in the stories of *al-Ḥiṣrim* and *Taksīr Rukab*. Both collections present formal characteristics that make them stand out amongst the works of the later period for the greater degree of textual unity the stories display. In *al-Ḥiṣrim*, multiple points of view on masculinity and the social and political dimension of gender roles emerge, while in *Taksīr Rukab* a greater presence of transgressive sexual images typifies most stories. The analysis has also highlighted how the prominent presence of this trope, however, has also resulted in an exaggerated sexualization of female characters, particularly in the two later collections. The marginal and accessory role women played in the early stories has been elevated to portray female protagonists who possess greater agency in their relationship with men; however, the form of power they have attained resides mostly in their increased bodily dimension. The transformation of female characters from objects of male lust, or simply victims of a patriarchal order, into sassy lustful subjects often serves the purpose of highlighting the male's incapacity. By contrast, females' social and political dimension is confined more often than not to the sexual weapon they can wield against their male counterparts. In addition, amongst the significant taboo-breaking images *Taksīr Rukab* contains, a few significant stories feature instances of same-sex intercourse which, in line with a widespread trend in contemporary Arabic literature, is never represented as a genuine form of love and affection. Akin to the representations of female protagonists' confidently performing their sexuality, homosexuality also functions as a device to expose the male's diminished self-worth and to denounce authoritarian practices as the result of an internalized form of submission to abuse amongst men.

This book has shown the applicability of an approach to contemporary Arabic literature that brings together a variety of subjects to substantiate a main argument about changing representations of gender roles. Coming to these conclusions would have proven complicated without the assistance of studies devoted to the history of Syria and the broader Arab world, social studies on sexuality and authoritarianism, and the capacity to access resources in a variety of languages. Making a virtue out of necessity, this approach was dictated primarily by the relative scarcity of resources focusing specifically on the same interstice between aesthetics, gender, ideology and authoritarianism. This methodology has also uncovered the potential for future research that a widely unexplored field like Syrian contemporary literature presents. In particular, the variety of responses that the connivance between authoritarianism, sectarianism and political Islam – an interstice that figures rarely in Tamir's stories in which the sectarian affiliation of the protagonists, especially minorities, is hardly mentioned or even hinted at – has generated in novelists and short-story writers in Syria since the early 2000s represents an intriguing area of investigation which remains largely uncharted.

Appendix

Appendix 1.1

The following chart illustrates in detail the dates of original publication for Tamir's short stories between 1958 and 1978. The chart also indicates the collection in which each individual short story appeared, highlighting sometimes a time lapse of a decade between the stories' original publication and their appearance in a particular compilation. [1]

Journal/magazine	Short story's title in Arabic	Date of original publication	Collection
al-Nuqqād (renamed al-Nāqid after 1960)	Rajul min Dimashq	1957	*Ṣahīl al-jawād al-abyaḍ* (1960)
	al-Ṣayf	1958	*Ṣahīl al-jawād al-abyaḍ* (1960)
al-Thaqāfa	al-Qabw	June 1958	*Ṣahīl al-jawād al-abyaḍ* (1960)
	al-Nujūm fawq al-ghāba	July 1959	*Ṣahīl al-jawād al-abyaḍ* (1960)
	al-Kanz	January 1959	*Ṣahīl al-jawād al-abyaḍ* (1960)
	al-Layl fī al-madīna	February 1960	*Ṣahīl al-jawād al-abyaḍ* (1960)
	Rabīʿ fī al-ramād	April 1960	*Rabīʿ fī al-ramād* (1963)
	Ḥaql al-banafsaj	July 1960	*Dimashq al-ḥarāʾiq* (1973)
	al-Jarīma	Oct–Nov 1961	*Rabīʿ fī al-ramād* (1963)
	Shams ṣaghīra	December 1961	*Rabīʿ fī al-ramād* (1963)
	Jankīz Khān	March 1962	*Rabīʿ fī al-ramād* (1963)

(*Continued*)

Journal/magazine	Short story's title in Arabic	Date of original publication	Collection
al-Ādāb	al-Rajul al-zanjī	April 1958	*Ṣahīl al-jawād al-abyaḍ* (1960)
	Ibtasim ya wajha-ha al-mut'ab	February 1959	*Ṣahīl al-jawād al-abyaḍ* (1960)
	Ṣahīl al-jawād al-abiyaḍ	May 1959	*Ṣahīl al-jawād al-abyaḍ* (1960)
	al-Ughniya al-zarqā' al-khashina	June 1959	*Ṣahīl al-jawād al-abyaḍ* (1960)
	al-Nahr mayyit	August 1959	*Ṣahīl al-jawād al-abyaḍ* (1960)
	Qaranfula lil-asfalt al-mut'ab	November 1959	*Ṣahīl al-jawād al-abyaḍ* (1960)
	Raḥīl ila al-baḥr	November 1960	*Dimashq al-ḥarā'iq* (1973)
	Wajh al-qamar	August 1962	*Dimashq al-ḥarā'iq* (1973)
	al-Badawī	October 1962	*Dimashq al-ḥarā'iq* (1973)
	al-A'dā'	April 1973	*al-Numūr fī al-yawm al-'āshir* (1978)
al-Ma'rifa	al-Aṭfāl	January 1964	*al-Ra'd* (1970)
	Jū'	January 1966	*al-Ra'd* (1970)
	al-Sijn	August 1966	*al-Ra'd* (1970)
	al-Ṣaqr	May 1968	*al-Ra'd* (1970)
	Alladhī aḥraqa al-sufun	September 1968	*al-Ra'd* (1970)
	Fī layla min al-layālī	February 1969	*al-Numūr fī al-yawm al-'āshir* (1978)
	Wajh al-qamar	May 1973	*Dimashq al-ḥarā'iq* (1973)
	al-Shajara al-Khaḍrā'	February 1973	*Dimashq al-ḥarā'iq* (1973)
	Randa	April 1974	*al-Numūr fī al-yawm al-'āshir* (1978)
	al-Zahra	February 1975	*al-Numūr fī al-yawm al-'āshir* (1978)
	al-Sahra	April 1976	*al-Numūr fī al-yawm al-'āshir* (1978)
	al-Farīsa	September 1977	*al-Numūr fī al-yawm al-'āshir* (1978)
	al-Mā' wa al-nār	July 1973	*Dimashq al-ḥarā'iq* (1973)

(*Continued*)

al-mawqif al-adabī	al-Bustān	Sept–Oct 1971	*Dimashq al-ḥarā'iq* (1973)
	al-Rāya al-sawdā'	June 1971	*Dimashq al-ḥarā'iq* (1973)
	al-Istighātha	September 1972	*Dimashq al-ḥarā'iq* (1973)
	al-Khirāf	Feb–Mar 1973	*Dimashq al-ḥarā'iq* (1973)
	Ya ayyuhā al-karaz al-mansī	July 1973	*Dimashq al-ḥarā'iq* (1973)
	Mā ḥadatha fī al-madīna allatī kānat nā'ima	January 1973	*al-Numūr fī al-yawm al-'āshir* (1978)
	al-Ibtisāma	April 1974	*al-Numūr fī al-yawm al-'āshir* (1978)
	al-Ightiyāl	August 1974	*al-Numūr fī al-yawm al-'āshir* (1978)
al-Hilāl	Shams ṣaghīra	August 1969	*Rabī' fī al-ramād* (1963)
	al-'Urs al-sharqī	August 1969	*al-Ra'd* (1970)
Jarīdat al-Kifāḥ	Imra'a waḥīda	1961	*Dimashq al-ḥarā'iq* (1973)
	Thalj ākhir al-layl	1961	*Rabī' fī al-ramād* (1963)
al-Ḥurriyya	al-Qurṣān	1961	*Rabī' fī al-ramād* (1963)
al-Majalla	al-I'dām	1970	*Dimashq al-ḥarā'iq* (1973)
Shi'r	al-Liḥā	April 1967	*al-Ra'd* (1970)

Appendix 1.2

The following is the story ‘One Night’, from *al-Numūr fī al-yawm al-ʿāshir* (Beirut, Dār al-Ādāb, 1978), pp. 32–45. Translated from Arabic by Alessandro Columbu.

One night (في ليلة من الليالي)

As the night’s black blanket falls upon the city, Abu Hasan wanders off from his dull neighbourhood, with its curvy dark alleys, its skinny people, its shabby houses stuck next to each other and its café which looked like a coffin made of worn wood. As he emerges to the broad roads, Abu Hasan is stunned by the racket, the fast cars, the fancy people and the multi-coloured, bright lights around him. He walks slowly, in stupor, his back straight and his head held high. His face is creased, but he is very proud of his thick moustache which elicits the curiosity and astonishment of many of those who look at him.

Indeed! You’re Abu Hasan and you deserve the admiration and the respect that you get. You’re a great man. Your dagger is a strike of lightning that anticipates a downpour of blood. Your heart is made of silver, and your hands of mountain rock. You’re unlike any other man. When you’re joyful you’re like a green orchard. When you’re angry death carries its empty casket and awaits the victim’s corpse. You’re a loyal lover. No cheating. No lies. No hypocrisy and no flattery from you. You call a spade a spade. If you beat someone, you make them bleed but never kill them. You make your enemies disappear, but you give yourself wholeheartedly to your friends. You’re in your forties, but when your body meets that of a woman’s, you remain in her blood until her death. You drink arak like it’s water and don’t get drunk. You engage in bloody fights as though you were smoking a cigarette by a riverbank. When you sing in your coarse voice you make rocks cry. You enjoy the secret respect and admiration of every man, woman and child in your street. When a woman from your neighbourhood argues with her husband, she doesn’t go to her family’s house to whine, she comes to you confident that whatever injustice has befallen her will certainly be unravelled. The kids in your neighbourhood love you, and they come to you crying for your help when their mothers beat them. If two friends fall out, you’re the only one whose words can rekindle their friendship. If an orphan wanted to get married, you act as his own family. You always take the side of the weak and oppressed, and you confront their victimizers. Never in your life have you bowed to humiliation and degradation.

Abu Hasan smiles proudly and happily as he carries on walking slowly amongst men without moustaches, and women who walk haughtily and elegantly with their head held high, pretty and perfumed like expensive dolls. Look . . . look Abu Hasan! Men look like women, and women look like men. But you're indifferent to all this. That's life. Nothing is eternal and every era has its men and women.

Two young girls appear before Abu Hasan, they're prettier than the morning jasmine. They look at his moustache in disbelief, making him even prouder of his facial hair which he strikes with his right hand in a haughty gesture. The two girls whisper something to each other then they burst out laughing derisively. Abu Hasan is rattled. He carries himself away from the two girls into a sideroad illuminated by electric lamps hanging from wooden lampposts. You?! You're Abu Hasan! You don't shy away like a little girl when someone mocks you. What a time we live in, where dogs bark at their owners.

Abu Hasan heard a song coming from an open window. He stopped and leaned against a tree. The singer's voice was raucous, the lyrics obscure, he sounded like the shrill of a bird that suddenly lost its wings and plummeted into a bottomless pit.

Abu Hasan imagined if the two girls got kidnapped. They would have to dance naked and in terror in a room full of men with thick moustaches and voracious eyes. He remembered a pretty woman from his neighbourhood who used to say to him: 'Marry me, and I will be your servant.' But one morning wailings and lamentations emerged from her house, wrapping the entire neighbourhood and its people in black. Abu Hasan didn't walk behind her coffin. He hid himself in his room, and buried his face in a pillow, unable to cry. His hoarse laments rose now and again raucous, sadder than a mother's weeping for the death of her daughter.

Suddenly, Abu Hasan heard a sharp cry for help, and saw a man running in his direction. He heard people yelling that he was a thief, urging everybody to catch him. Abu Hasan tried to grab him, but the thief dodged him skilfully and resumed his running, leaving behind whatever fell off his hands. Abu Hasan picked it up. It was a woman's handbag. He looked at it and said to himself:

- 'What would people in my neighbourhood say if they saw me carrying a woman's item?'

Those who'd been chasing the robber came up to Abu Hasan, accompanied by a chubby police officer.

- 'I'm sorry', said Abu Hasan, 'that devil was like mercury, I couldn't catch him'.

A woman pointed in Abu Hassan's direction shouting at the other people:

- 'Get him, he stole my bag. Look! He still has it!'

Abu Hassan replied:

- 'Shame on you, woman, what are you on about?'

The woman snatched the handbag from Abu Hassan's hands and exclaimed:

- 'Watch out, he's running away!'

The cop and a bunch of other people quickly grabbed Abu Hassan.

- 'Go on then', said the cop.
- 'Where?' asked him Abu Hassan

'Where?' the cop replied, 'To the police station of course. Perhaps you were thinking we'd take you to a nightclub?'

Abu Hassan tried to retort, but the insults and the slurs made him go silent. He walked alongside the cop, surrounded by a group of men, women and children pointing their fingers at him and calling him a thief in a loud voice.

At the nearest police station, Abu Hassan was taken immediately to see the chief, a young clean-shaven fellow with a nice white face and stern, forbidding eyes, sitting behind a desk upon which lay papers and a phone.

The cop approached the chief and stood at attention. He greeted him with his hand; then relayed what had just occurred.

Abu Hasan intervened:

- 'None of what he said is true.'

'Quiet', said the chief, 'talk only if I say so'.

The woman shouted again:

- 'He stole my handbag and ran away!'

She was joined by all the other people:

- 'We all saw him, we chased him and caught him.'
- 'I caught him with the bag still in his hand, Sir', said the cop.

The chief remained silent at first. Then he cast an inquiring look at Abu Hasan and said to him in contempt: 'Please . . . it's your turn, let's hear your eloquence. What's up? Did you swallow your tongue, you crook?'

- 'I'm not a crook', said Abu Hasan.
- 'So, who are you?' the chief snapped at him, 'perhaps a mosque sheikh without us knowing?'
- 'I'm a man', said Abu Hasan, 'and men don't rob women'.

The chief sprang up from his chair and approached Abu Hasan.

- 'Blimey!' said the chief mockingly, 'you're not just a crook, you're an impudent one too'.
- 'I didn't steal the handbag', said Abu Hasan. 'I saw it falling from the thief's hands and I picked it up.'
- 'Listen, denial won't do you any good, you better confess what you did now, or you will regret your mother brought you to life.'

Abu Hasan clutched his moustache with his left hand:

- 'May this be a woman's moustache if I'm lying.'
- 'To hell with your moustache', said the chief, 'I don't have time for banter. Speak now or I'll smash your head.'

Abu Hasan's face turned red as he retorted:

- 'The man who smashes my head is yet to be born. Ask people from my street and you will find out who's Abu Hasan.'

The chief grew furious and said:

- 'Why you dog! . . . confess or I'll beat you and your neighbours with my shoe!'
- 'There isn't much more to say' – said Abu Hassan – 'just be a real man, a man who knows another man's worth.'

The chief shook his head and spoke, trying to remain calm.

- 'You really need to be taught a lesson, but you've come to the right place cause I know how to deal with people like you.'

He turned to the chubby cop and commanded him:

- 'Go get me a pair of scissors, chop-chop.'

'Yes sir', said the cop before he dashed out.

The chief returned to his desk. He sat down with a frown on his face and pressed a button. A yellow-faced cop appeared, and the chief ordered him to take down the testimonies from the woman and the other witnesses. 'Yes sir!', said the cop.

They left and chief remained alone with Abu Hassan. Abu Hassan's voice trembled as he said to the chief 'Look at me, how could I be a thief who robs women?'

The chief didn't say anything, but his expression hardened; he picked up the phone and brought it to his mouth. He spoke in a low voice and put the receiver down. He sat and glared at Abu Hassan, who just stood there, upset and confused.

The chubby cop returned holding a large pair of scissors, followed by more cops who glared at Abu Hassan with disdain and contempt. The chief sprang from his chair and beamed as he put his hands on the scissors.

'Hold this dog for me, will you?' said the chief to the other cops as he pointed his scissors at Abu Hassan.

- 'Who are you calling a dog you half man you, sod off!' bellowed Abu Hassan as he lunged at the chief fumingly.

It was just a second before the other cops grabbed him. Abu Hassan tried to sneak away from them, but their blows and their kicks began raining down on him. They beat him with such brutality and hatred as if he had slaughtered their own mothers. They kept giving it to him until he could no longer put up with it and his body looked like a shabby piece of fabric.

'Hold him up for me', said the chief. 'He's still moving', he said to the chubby cop. 'Hold his head up or I'll give *you* the bastinado.'

The cop proceeded to grab Abu Hassan's hair and pulled his head back violently, making Abu Hassan's face an easy prey.

The chief approached him with a smile, holding the scissors in his hand.

- 'Now you will pay for your insults, and you will see what a half-a-man is capable of.'

Abu Hassan tried to get away from the officers' hold with terror blazing in his eyes as the scissors came closer to his moustache. He was unable to move as they held him firmly.

- 'By God, I'm innocent!', he yelled.

As the scissors closed in on his moustache he was gripped by fear and screamed again:

- 'Please!'
- 'Say that you stole the handbag and you won't get hurt.'

Silence reigned in the room for a moment, then Abu Hassan murmured:

- 'I stole the handbag from the woman.'

The chief of the police station laughed:

- 'How long will this country have people like you?' he said in disdain.

The scissors descended on Abu Hassan's moustache and operated patiently and with great satisfaction as he let out a long, hoarse scream.

The chief threw the scissors on his desk and said to his men: 'What? Are you touched by his screaming? Make him stop!'

They pounced on him again with the fiercest beating until he collapsed. Abu Hassan was still able to yell his insults at them. They took off his shoes and lifted his legs up, then proceeded to batter his soles with a sharp stick.

Abu Hassan yelled at the cops:

- 'Why you sons of bitches I'll kill you even if that's the last thing I do with my life!'
- 'Keep giving it to him until he shuts his mouth, I don't want to hear his voice', said the chief.

Abu Hassan bit his lower lip, holding the pain and the screams that he'd have wanted to let out at the top of his lungs.

'Leave him', said the chief to his men. Then, he turned to Abu Hassan and said: 'Get up and stand on your feet.'

Abu Hassan gathered his strength to stand up and followed the chief's instructions. 'Pick up your shoes', said the chief to Abu Hassan. Quietly groaning in pain Abu Hassan obeyed again, and stood up with his back bent, holding a shoe in each hand.

- 'Say Abu Hassan', asked him the chief, 'are you a man or a woman?'
- 'Of course, I'm a man', replied Abu Hassan.
- 'Liar. You're a woman. Go on. Say that you're a woman. I will be furious if you don't admit that you're a woman. You know what happens when I get angry.'
- 'I am . . . a woman', Abu Hassan faltered in an inaudible voice.

The chief snapped at him. 'I didn't hear you. Speak up! Do you think you're whispering into your girlfriend's ears?'

- 'I'm a woman', said Abu Hassan in a loud voice, looking down.

The chief laughed boisterously. 'Be grateful that we're not *homosexuals* here', he added making the officers burst out laughing.

'Take him', said the chief in a disgusted tone. 'I'll be done with him later.'

The officers dragged Abu Hassan out, kicking, slapping and insulting him. They took him to one of the cells and locked the door. It was an empty cell with no windows and a dim-lighted lamp hanging from the roof. Abu Hassan collapsed on the floor groaning and in pain when suddenly he heard someone's sharp voice asking him: 'Did they beat you a lot? Don't be upset . . . it's the only form of amusement they know.'

Abu Hassan raised his head quizzically and saw a twelve-year-old boy sitting on the ground, leaning on the wall of the cell. 'What are you doing here?' Abu Hassan asked him in bewilderment.

- 'They caught me', said the kid pointing at the door.
- 'What did you do?'
- 'I didn't do anything.'
- 'They arrested you because you didn't do anything?'
- 'I murdered my mother.'
- 'Goddamn . . . come again?!'
- 'I murdered my mother, slaughtered her. Not even a hungry dog would eat the food she made.'

The kid laughed cheerfully; he pointed at the door again and added,

- 'These poor devils went through the roof cause they kept looking for the knife but they couldn't find it.'

Abu Hassan thought that he was asleep and that the whole thing was a terrifying nightmare. He stared at the kid in silence, oblivious for a second to the excruciating pain in his flesh and his bones. The kid had a meek expression in his face, and long black straight hair.

- 'I wanna sleep', the kid said.
- 'No one is stopping you', Abu Hassan.
- 'My mother usually tells me a story before I go to sleep.'
- 'Shut your mouth and sleep.'
- 'Tell me a story.'

Abu Hassan was speechless; he stared at the kid.

- 'If you tell me a story', said the kid to Abu Hassan, 'I will give you a knife that kills a hundred people.'

Abu Hassan was dumbfounded. The kid removed one of his shoes and produced long knife with dry blood stains on its sharp blade. The kid showed it to Abu Hassan: 'What . . .? you thought I was lying?'

Abu Hassan extended his hand towards the kid and said to him in a commanding voice: 'Give it to me.'

The kid gave him the knife. Abu Hassan caressed its handle eagerly with his fingers.

The kid lay on the ground and implored Abu Hassan again: 'Go on, tell me a story.'

Abu Hassan started monotonously: 'Once upon a time, there was a guy called Mustafa. He was a poor man, the only thing he owned in this world was his moustache, until one day the king ordered all the men in his kingdom shave their moustache. All the men shaved except for Mustafa, who refused to give up on his moustache. He was arrested, beaten and humiliated, and incarcerated. One day Mustafa was summoned to appear before the king to be punished.'

'Why did you disobey me?' asked him the king. 'Do you know what happens to those who ignore my orders?'

'Your majesty can do with me whatever he pleases,' said Mustafa, 'but I'd rather be decapitated than shave my moustache.'

The king smiled cunningly and then said,

- 'I'll give you a thousand dinar if you shave it.'
- 'No.'
- 'Don't be stubborn. Listen here, you want more? I'll give you a million dinars.'
- 'All the gold in the world isn't worth a hair of a man's moustache.'
- 'I'll make you a minister.'
- 'No.'
- 'I will appoint you Grand Vizier of my kingdom.'
- 'I'd rather be a beggar', said Mustafa. 'A beggar with a moustache is worth more than a Grand Vizier without one.'
- 'I'll make you my partner in government', said the King. 'You will rule over my kingdom like I do.'

Mustafa didn't yield. The king shook his head and pondered for a while. 'You're truly a man, you have proven that you're the only real man in my kingdom. Not only you can keep your moustache, but I will also reward you in the best way possible.'

The king married off his pretty daughter to Mustafa, and he loved her deeply. They lived together happily for months until one day Mustafa woke up to find that she was frowning and in a bad mood. 'What is it?' he asked her.

- 'What is it? You of all people should know', she snapped at him.
- 'Me? I'd never want to upset you', he said. 'Ask me anything you want, and I'll gladly do it for you.'
- 'I can't stand your moustache', she said. 'You'd look a lot prettier, and I'd love you much more if you shaved it.'

Mustafa was annoyed at her request; he tried to convince her of the absurdity of her words, but she stood her ground and said to him: 'I never want to see you again unless you shave your moustache.' The king's daughter kept her word and she locked herself up in her chamber.

Mustafa suffered, depriving himself of his beloved. He remained patient and resilient for a long time until he gave in and surrendered to his own heart. He shaved his moustache and ran to the king's daughter's chamber.

'Open up', he said as he knocked on her door. 'I did as you said.'

She opened the door but as soon as she laid her eyes on him, she was taken aback by his sight, and she burst out laughing. Mustafa moved towards her eagerly and tried to hug her, but she sneaked away and said to him drily:

- 'Don't you dare come near me.'
- 'Why?' Mustafa asked her.
- 'Go look at yourself in the mirror if you wanna know why. Your face without a moustache is hilarious; all the jesters in my father's kingdom cannot compete with you. You're ugly too. Even an old decrepit dog would find you repulsive.'

Mustafa was devastated. He took out his dagger and stabbed himself in the heart as he gave the king's daughter one final stern look of love.

Mustafa staggered, as he was about to collapse and die. 'Watch out!' she reproached him. 'You're gonna stain my bedcover with your blood!'

. . . and when people found out what had happened to Mustafa they were saddened, and they wept.' . . .

Abu Hassan finished his story and looked at the kid. He was stretched on the floor of the cell with his eyes closed, peacefully surrendering to a deep slumber, as his fingers pressing on the knife's handle grew more and more vicious.

The knife moved slowly towards the kid; then it stopped and it trembled angrily, hesitating between Abu Hassan's heart and the kid's neck.

Notes

Introduction

1 General overviews of Arabic literature connecting literary production to historical and socio-political developments: Mustafa M. Badawi, ed., *Modern Arabic Literature* (Cambridge: Cambridge University Press, 1992); Angelika Neuwirth, Andreas Pflitsch and Barbara Winckler, eds, *Arabic Literature: Postmodern Perspectives* (London: Saqi Books, 2010); Paul Starkey, *Modern Arabic Literature* (Edinburgh: Edinburgh University Press, 2006); On the Arabic short story, see Sabry Hafiz, *The Quest for Identities – The Development of the Modern Arabic Short Story* (London: Saqi Books, 2007). On the Arabic novel, see Roger Allen, *The Arabic Novel – An Historical and Critical Introduction* (Manchester: The University of Manchester, 1982). For monographies of individual authors: Paul Starkey, *Sonallah Ibrahim – Rebel with a Pen* (Edinburgh: Edinburgh University Press, 2016). For the development of gender representations: Kifah Hanna, *Feminism and Avant-Garde Aesthetics in the Levantine Novel* (New York: Palgrave Macmillan, 2016).

2 Stefan G. Meyer, *The Experimental Arabic Novel – Postcolonial Literary Modernism in the Levant* (New York: State University of New York Press, 2001), 97–8; Mohja Kahf, 'The Silences of Contemporary Syrian Literature', *World Literature Today* 2 (Spring 2001): 224–36.

3 For examples of works that address Syrian literature and cultural production specifically, see Samira Aghacy, *Masculine Identity in the Fiction of the Arab East Since 1967* (Syracuse: Syracuse University Press, 2009); Edward Ziter, *Political Performance in Syria – From the Six-Day War to the Syrian Uprising* (New York: Palgrave Macmillan, 2015); Alexa Firat and R. Shareah Taleghani, eds, *Generations of Dissent – Intellectuals, Cultural Production, and the State in the Middle East and North Africa* (Syracuse: Syracuse University Press, 2020); Rebecca Joubin, *Mediating the Uprising: Narratives of Gender and Marriage in Syrian Television Drama* (New Brunswick: Rutgers University Press, 2020).

4 Sabry Hafez, 'The Modern Arabic Short Story', in *Modern Arabic Literature*, ed. Mustafa M. Badawi (Cambridge: Cambridge University Press, 1992), 270–328; Ṣabrī Ḥāfiẓ, 'Zakariyyā Tamir shāʿir al-qiṣṣa al-ʿarabīyya', afterword to *Aff!*

Zakariyyā Tamir - Mukhtārāt qiṣaṣiyyah (Cairo: Al-hay'a al-ʿāmma la-quṣūr al-thaqāfa, 1998), 285–346; Ulrike Stehli-Werbeck, 'The Poet of the Arabic Short Story: Zakariyya Tamir', in *Arabic Literature: Postmodern Perspectives*, Angelika Neuwirth, Andreas Pflitsch and Barbara Winckler, eds, 220–30.

5 Raymond Williams, *Marxism and Literature* (Oxford: Oxford University Press, 1977); Terry Eagleton, *Marxism and Literary Criticism* (Berkeley and Los Angeles: University of California Press, 1976); Terry Eagleton, *Literary Theory – An Introduction* (Oxford: Blackwell Publishing, 1983).

[18] Ibid., 128–35.

6 Kamal Abu Deeb, 'The Collapse of Totalizing Discourse and the Rise of Marginalized/Minority Discourses', in *Tradition, Modernity and Postmodernity in Arabic Literature – Essays in Honour of Professor Issa J. Boullata*, ed. Wael Hallaq and Kamal Abdel-Malek (Leiden-Boston-Köln: Brill, 2000), 335–66.

7 Ibid., 351.

8 Zakariyyā Tamir, *Ṣahīl al-jawād al-abyaḍ* (Beirut: Dār majallat al-Shiʿr, 1960).

9 Zakariyyā Tamir, *Rabīʾ fī al-Ramād* (Damascus: Wizārat al-Thaqāfa, 1963).

10 Zakariyyā Tamir, *al-Raʿd* (Damascus: Ittiḥād al-kuttāb al-ʿarab, 1970).

11 Zakariyyā Tamir, *Dimashq al-ḥarāʾiq* (Damascus: Ittiḥād al-kuttāb al-ʿarab, 1973).

12 Zakariyyā Tamir, *al-Numūr fī al-yawm al-ʿāshir* (Beirut: Dār al-Ādāb, 1978).

13 Zakariyyā Tamir, *Nidāʾ Nūḥ* (London: Riyad el-Rayyes books, 1994).

14 Zakariyyā Tamir, *Sa-naḍḥak* (London: Riyad el-Rayyes books, 1998).

15 Zakariyyā Tamir, *al-Ḥiṣrim* (London: Riyad el-Rayyes books, 2000).

16 Zakariyyā Tamir, *Taksīr Rukab* (London: Riyad el-Rayyes books, 2002).

17 See for example Roger Allen, 'Literary History and the Arab Novel', *World Literature Today* 2 (Spring, 2001): 205–13; Others, however, have also stressed the oversimplified nature of this demarcation. See Starkey, *Modern Arabic Literature*, 139.

18 See for example Hafez, 'The Modern Arabic Short Story'; Ḥāfiẓ, 'Zakariyyā Tamir shāʿir al-qiṣṣa al-ʿarabīyya'; Stehli-Werbeck, 'The Poet of the Arabic Short Story', 220–30.

19 See for example: Evelyne Accad, *Veil of Shame: The Role of Women in Contemporary Fiction of North Africa and the Arab World* (Québec: Éditions Naaman, 1978); Margot Badran and miriam cooke, eds, *Opening the Gates: A Century of Arab Feminist Writing* (London: Virago Press ltd., 1990).

20 Aghacy, *Masculine Identity in the Fiction of the Arab East Since 1967*, 130.

21 R.W. Connell, *Masculinities* (Berkeley: University of California Press, 2005). R.W. Connell and James Messerschmidt, 'Hegemonic Masculinity: Rethinking the Concept', *Gender and Society* 19, no. 6 (2005): 829–59.

22 Connell, *Masculinities*, 77–81.
23 Ibid., 79–80.
24 Ibid., 78.
25 Kahf, 'The Silences of Contemporary Syrian Literature', 230.
26 R.W. Connell, *Gender and Power* (Stanford: Stanford University Press, 1987), 183.
27 Connell and Messerschmidt, 'Hegemonic Masculinity', 849.
28 Hisham Sharabi, *Neopatriarchy – A Theory of Distorted Change in Arab Society* (Oxford: Oxford University Press 1988), 97.
29 Halim Barakat, *The Arab World – Society, Culture, and State* (Berkeley: University of California Press, 1993), 97–118.
30 Mordechai Kedar, *Asad in Search of Legitimacy – Message and Rhetoric in the Syrian Press under Hafiz and Bashar* (Brighton: Sussex Academic Press, 2005), 21.
31 Lisa Wedeen, *Ambiguities of Domination: Politics, Rhetoric, and Symbols in Contemporary Syria* (Chicago: University of Chicago Press, 1999), 49.
32 Fatima Mernissi, *Beyond the Veil – Male-female Dynamics in Modern Muslim Societies* (Bloomington and Indianapolis: Indiana University Press, 1987); Nawāl al-Saʿadāwī, *al-Marʾa wa al-jins* (Beirut: al-muʾassasa al-ʿarabiyya lil-dirāsāt wa al-nashr, 1974).
33 Mernissi, *Beyond the Veil*, 27.
34 See Nikki R. Keddie, *Women in the Middle East – Past and Present* (Princeton: Princeton University Press, 2007), 17, 37–9.
35 Eagleton, *Marxism and Literary Criticism*, 15–17.
36 Aghacy, *Masculine Identity in the Fiction of the Arab East Since 1967*, 2.
37 Emma Westney, 'Individuation and literature: Zakariyya Tamir and his Café Man', in *Marginal Voices in Literature and Society: Individual and Society in the Mediterranean Muslim World*, ed. Robin Ostle dir. (Strasbourg: European Science Foundation (ESF), in collaboration with the Maison Méditerranéenne des Sciences de l'Homme d'Aix-en-Provence, 2000), 191.

Chapter 1

1 Dima Alchukr, 'Interview with Zakaria Tamer', *Banipal* 53 (Summer 2015): 116.
2 Zakariyyā Tamir, 'Qaranfula lil-asfalt al-mutʿab', *al-Ādāb* 11 (1959): 40; Tamir, *Ṣahīl al-jawād al-abyaḍ*, 108. All translations from Arabic are mine unless otherwise noted.

3 Sami M. Moubayed, *Steel & Silk: Men and Women who Shaped Syria 1900–2000* (Seattle: Cune Press, 2005), 264.

4 Soraya Botrous, *Les Influences Occidentales sur la nouvelle en Syrie Depuis 1946* (PhD dissertation, University of Paris-Sorbonne, December 1987), 107.

5 Mustafa Badawi, 'Commitment in Contemporary Arabic Literature', in *Critical Perspectives on Modern Arabic Literature 1945–1980*, ed. Issa J. Boullata (Washington: Three Continents Press, 1980), 23–44.

6 Edward W. Said, 'Arabic Prose and Prose Fiction after 1948', in *Reflections on Exile and Other Literary and Cultural Essays*, ed. Edward W. Said (London: Granta Books, 2001), 46.

7 This monthly periodical is still published to this day and its full archive is available on www.al-adab.com. Significantly, its slogan has remained remindful of its initial mission: '*akthar ḥadātha*[tan]*, ashadd iltizām*[an]' ('more modern, more strongly committed').

8 Suhayl Idrīs, 'Risālat al-Ādāb', *al-Ādāb* 1 (January 1953): 1.

9 Monica Ruocco, *L'intellettuale arabo tra impegno e dissenso – Analisi della rivista libanese al-Ādāb (1953–1994)* (Rome: Jouvence, 1999), 51.

10 Alexa Firat, 'Cultural Battles on the Literary Field: From the Syrian Writers' Collective to the Last Days of Socialist Realism in Syria', *Middle Eastern Literatures* 18, no. 2 (2015): 155.

11 Ibid., 158.

12 See Dīb, *Tārīkh Sūriyya al-muʿāṣir*, 117–44; 171–96.

13 'Abd al-Razzāq 'Īd, *al-'Ālam al-qiṣaṣī li-Zakariyyā Tamir* (Beirut: Dār al-farābī, 1989), 5. Quoted in Imtinān 'Uthmān al-Ṣamādī, *Zakariyyā Tamir wa al-qiṣṣa al-qaṣīra* ('Ammān: Wizārat al-Thaqāfa, 1995), 23.

14 Zakariyyā Tamir, 'Laysa bi-wazīr wa-lā bi-shāʿir', *al-Taḍāmun* 232 (1987): 66.

15 https://www.facebook.com/permalink.php?story_fbid=1166362166783621&id=222667394486441&comment_id=1166392723447232&comment_tracking=%7B%22tn%22%3A%22R%22%7D.

16 Dīb, *Tārīkh Sūriyya al-muʿāṣir*, 83.

17 Tamir, 'Laysa bi-wazīr wa-lā bi-shāʿir', 66.

18 Ḥāfiẓ, 'Zakariyyā Tamir shāʿir al-qiṣṣa al-ʿarabiyya', 290.

19 Muḥyī al-dīn Ṣubḥī, 'Muqābala maʿ Zakariyyā Tamir', *al-Maʿrifa* 126 (August 1972): 109–16.

20 Hafez, 'The Modern Arabic Short Story', 322–4.

21 Ibid., 317.

22 Frank O'Connor, *The Lonely Voice – A Study of the Short Story* (London: Macmillan and Co., 1963). Introduction, 13–45.

23 Ṣubḥī Ḥadīdī, 'Poet of the Short Story', *Banipal* 53 (Summer 2015): 74.

24 Meyer, *The Experimental Arabic Novel*, 15.

25 According to Syrian dissident intellectual Bourhan Ghalioun, 'it was Camus, and not Marx, the one intellectual that influenced revolutionaries the most in the Near East after 1950' in Bourhan Ghalioun, *La malaise arabe. L'état contre la nation* (Paris: La Découverte, 1991), 81.

26 Yoav Di-Capua, 'Arab Existentialism: A Lost Chapter in the Intellectual History of Decolonization', *American Historical Review* 17, no. 4 (October 2012): 1074.

27 Ruocco, *L'intellettuale arabo tra impegno e dissenso*, 79–84.

28 Firat, 'Cultural Battles on the Literary Field', 158.

29 Hafez, *The Quest for Identities*, 27.

30 Ḥannā Mīna, 'Fī al-tajriba al-riwā'iyya', *al-Ma'rifa* 224 (October 1980): 126.

31 Between 1920 and 1946 Syria was put under French mandate by the League of Nations. See Daniel Neep, *Occupying Syria under the French Mandate* (Cambridge: Cambridge University Press, 2012).

32 Ḥannā Mīna, *al-Maṣābīḥ al-zurq* (Beirut: Dār al-Ādāb, 1989. 1st edition, Beirut: Dar al-Fikr al-Jadıd̄, 1954).

33 Aḥmad Muḥammad al-'Aṭiyya, *al-Iltizām wa al-thawra fī al-adab al-'arabī al-ḥadīth* (Beirut: Dar al-'awda, 1974), 32–7.

34 Muḥammad Kāmil al-Khaṭīb, *'Ālam Ḥannā Mīna al-riwā'ī* (Beirut: Dār al-ādāb, 1979), 20–4.

35 Nabīl Sulaymān and Bū 'Alī Yāsīn, *al-Adab wa al-idıyūlūjıyā fī Sūriyya 1967–1973* (Beirut: Dār Ibn Khaldūn, 1974).

36 Ibid., 211.

37 Muḥammad Kāmil al-Khaṭīb, Nabīl Sulaymān and Bū 'Alī Yāsīn, eds, *Ma'ārik thaqāfiyya fī Sūriyya 1975–1977* (Beirut: Dār ibn Rushd, 1978).

38 Muḥammad Kāmil al-Khaṭīb, "Ālam Zakariyyā Tamir al-qiṣaṣī', *al-Ba'th*, 26 May 1977. Also in *Ma'ārik thaqāfiyya fī Sūriyya 1975–1977*, 167–74.

39 al-Khaṭīb, "Ālam Zakariyyā Tamir al-qiṣaṣī', 167.

40 Ibid., 169.

41 Ibid., 171.

42 Tamir, *al-Ra'd*, 19.

43 al-Khaṭīb, "Ālam Zakariyyā Tamir al-qiṣaṣī', 171.

44 Ibid., 172.

45 Hafez, 'The Modern Arabic Short Story', 299.

46 Jean-Paul Sartre, *Qu'est-ce que la littérature?* (Paris: Gallimard, 1948).

47 Ṭāhā Ḥusayn, 'al-Adīb yaktub[u] lil-khāṣṣa', *al-Ādāb*(5 (May 1955): 9–16.

48 Verena Klemm, 'Different Notions of Commitment (*iltizām*) and Committed Literature (*al-adab al-multazim*) in the literary circles of the Mashriq', *Arabic and Middle Eastern Literature* 3, no. 1 (2000): 57.

49 Badawi, 'Commitment in Contemporary Arabic Literature', 34.

50 With the term 'Arabstan' ('arabstān) the author here is referring to Iran's Khuzestan Province, where a sizeable Arabic-speaking community resides.

51 Zakariyyā Tamir, 'Ḥaky al-Udabā' al-Aṣfār', *al-Ba'ath*, 7 July 1975. Also in *Ma'ārik thaqāfiyya fī Sūriyya 1975–1977*, 38.

52 Ṣubḥī, 'Muqābala ma' Zakariyyā Tamir', 110.

53 Ibid. 110.

54 Ibid. 112.

55 Hafez, 'The Modern Arabic Short Story', 317.

56 Eagleton, *Marxism and Literary Criticism*, 16.

57 Ṣubḥī, 'Muqābala ma' Zakariyyā Tamir', 113.

58 Sulaymān and Yāsīn, *al-Adab wa al-idıyūlūjıyā*, 5–10.

59 Ibid., 212.

60 Ibid., 214.

61 Ibid., 213.

62 See for example Khaldūn al-Sham'a, 'Khams mulāḥaẓāt – fī al-minhaj al-tajrīdī al-lā wāqi'ī', *al-Ba'th*, 7 June 1977. Also in *Ma'ārik thaqāfiyya fī Sūriyya 1975–1977*, 175.

63 Abu Deeb, 'The Collapse of the Totalizing Discourse', 347.

64 Ibid., 338.

65 Kamal Abu Deeb, 'Cultural Creation in a Fragmented Society', in *The Next Arab Decade – Alternative Futures*, ed. Hisham Sharabi (Boulder and London: Westview/Mansell 1988), 175–6.

66 Stehli-Werbeck, 'The Poet of the Arabic Short Story', 220–30.

67 See in English: Zakaria Tamer, *Tigers on the Tenth Day and Other Stories*, trans. Denys Johnson-Davies (London, Melbourne, New York: Quartet Books, 1985).

68 Ibid., 80.

69 'Qirā'āt', *al-Ma'rifa*, 219 (May 1980): 5. Available at http://syrbook.gov.sy/old/img/uploads1/ma3refeh_archive_pdf20140720134510.pdf.

70 'al-Istibdād wa al-taraqqī' (Despotism and progress) in 'Abd al-Raḥmān al-Kawākibī, *al-A'māl al-kāmila lil-Kawākibī* (Beirut: Markaz dirāsāt al-waḥda al-'arabiyya, 1995), 313.

71 Alchukr, 'Interview with Zakaria Tamer', 130.

72 Ziad Majed, A dialogue with Zakaria Tamer', Available at https://freesyriantranslators.net/2012/07/22/a-dialogue-with-zakaria-tamer-2/, on 5 June 2015.

73 Ruocco, *L'intellettuale arabo tra impegno e dissenso*, 172.
74 Gilles Kepel et Yann Richard, eds, *Intellectuels et militants de l'Islam contemporain* (Paris: Seuil, 1990), 18.
75 Wedeen, *Ambiguities of Domination*, 33–66.
76 Andreas Pflitsch, 'The End of Illusions', in *Arabic Literature Postmodern Perspectives*, 25–37.
77 See also Frederick Pannewick, and Georges Khalil, eds, *Commitment and Beyond – Reflections on/of the Political in Arabic Literature since the 1940s* (Wiesbaden: Reichert Verlag 2015).
78 'Umar Qaddūr, 'al-Riwāya al-Sūriyya al-Jadīda: ẓāhira ibdā'iyya am ẓāhira i'lāmiyya?', *al-Ādāb* 9–10 (2009): 98–101.
79 Ibid., 99.
80 Khālid Khalīfa, *Madīḥ al-Karāhiya* (Damascus: Dār Amīsa, 2006).
81 Martina Censi, 'Tra critica sociale ed erotismo, un esempio della nuova narrativa siriana: *Ḥurrās al-hawā'* di Rūzā Yāsīn Ḥasan', *La rivista di ArabLit* 2 (2011): 21–38.
82 Max Weiss, 'Who Laughs Last', in *Middle East Authoritarianisms – Governance, Contestation and Resilience in Syria and Iran*, ed. Steven Heydemann and Reinoud Leenders (Stanford: Stanford University Press, 2013), 143–66.
83 al-Ṣamādī, *Zakariyyā Tamir wa al-qiṣṣa al-qaṣīra*, 27.
84 Zakariyya Tamir, *Hijā' al-qatīl li-qātilihi* (Beirut: Riyad el-Rayyes Books, 2003).
85 Zakariyya Tamir, *Arḍ al-wayl*, (Beirut: Jadāwil, 2015).
86 'The Biography', *Banipal*, 180–1.
87 'Jā'izat Maḥmūd Darwīsh li-Zakariyyā Tamir wa Hānī Abū As'ad', *al-Jazīra*, 15 March 2015. Available at https://goo.gl/BQEafS, on 15 March 2015.
88 Weiss, 'Who Laughs Last', 155.
89 David W. Lesch, *The New Lion of Damascus – Bashar al-Asad and Modern Syria* (New Haven and London: Yale University Press, 2005), 81.
90 Ibid., 92–7.
91 Tamir, *Taksīr Rukab*, 151.
92 Ibid., 153.
93 Ibid., 151.
94 Unpublished. Performed in 1979.
95 Jafrā Bahā', 'Muthaqqafūn wa fannānūn sūriyyūn ḍidda al-thawra', Available at https://www.alarabiya.net/articles/2012/05/14/214117.html, on 5 December 2013.
96 Samar Yazbik, *Taqāṭu' nīrān* (Beirut: Dār al-Ādāb, 2012).
97 Samar Yazbik, *Bawwābāt arḍ al-'adam* (Beirut: Dār al-Ādāb, 2015).
98 Muṣṭafā Khalīfa, *al-Qawqa'* (Beirut: Dār al-Ādāb, 2008).

99 R. Shareah Taleghani, 'Vulnerability and recognition in Syrian prison literature', *International Journal of Middle East Studies* 49 (2017): 102.

100 Some of Farzāt's cartoons are reproduced in Wedeen, *Ambiguities of Domination*, 134–43.

101 'Ali Ferzat: Cartoonist in Exile', Available at https://www.theguardian.com/world/2013/aug/19/ali-ferzat-cartoonist-exile-syria, on 5 January 2015.

102 Ziad Majed, 'A Dialogue with Zakaria Tamer'.

103 Ibid.

104 Wedeen, *Ambiguities of Domination*, 73–5.

105 Available at http://ziadmajed.blogspot.co.uk/2012/06/blog-post_3737.html.

106 See for example Haytham Ḥusayn, 'Istīṭān al-khawf: al-muthaqqaf al-'arabī al-madh'ūr' (Settling fear: the paranoid Arab intellectual), *al-'Arab*, 8 June 2014, Available at http://alarab.co.uk/?id=24710; Mu'in al-Bayārī, 'Zakariyyā Tamir . . . al-wisām thumma al-hijā"(Zakariyyā Tamir . . . the decoration, and then the satire), *Ṣafḥāt sūriyya*, 6 May 2012, Available at https://goo.gl/FM26cL.

107 Tamir has denied the political nature of the award, which in his opinion is granted to truly meritorious writers. See Galdini and Columbu, On the side of the Syrian People, in al-Jazeera, https://www.aljazeera.com/indepth/features/2017/08/zakaria-tamer-side-syrian-people-170822130848510.html.

108 Kahf, 'The Silences of Contemporary Syrian Literature', 233.

Chapter 2

1 Joseph Massad, 'Conceiving the Masculine: Gender and Palestinian Nationalism', *Middle East Journal* 3 (Summer 1995): 467–83.

2 Certain parts of this chapter are adapted from my article 'Hadatha, Dissent and Hegemonic Masculinity in the Short Stories of Zakariyya Tamir' included in the edited volume *Generations of Dissent: Intellectuals, Cultural Production, and the State in the Middle East and North Africa*, ed. Alexa Firat and R. Shareah Taleghani (Syracuse: Syracuse University Press, 2020).

3 Abu Deeb, 'The Collapse of the Totalizing Discourse', 344–5.

4 Ibid., 343.

5 Mohammad Shaheen, *The Modern Arabic Short Story – Shahrazad Returns* (London: Macmillan Press, 1989), 71.

6 Aghacy, *Masculine Identity in the Fiction of the Arab East Since 1967*, 56.

7 Abu Deeb, 'The Collapse of the Totalizing Discourse', 346.

8 See Hanna Batatu, *Syria's Peasantry, the Descendants of its Lesser Rural Notables, and Their Politics*, (Princeton: Princeton University Press, 1999), 131–75.

9 Tamir, *Rabī' fī al-Ramād*, 32.

10 Tamir, *al-Ra'd*, 13.

11 Zakariyyā Tamir, 'al-Qabw', *al-Thaqāfa* 2 (1958): 48.

12 Ibid., 50.

13 Ibid. 51.

14 Zakariyyā Tamir, 'al-Badawī', *al-Ādāb* 10 (1962): 21–4, 52–6.

15 This name recurs frequently in Tamir's stories; for example, in 'Wajh al-qamar', a story relevant for the originally female point of view on sexuality it proposes, the name of the protagonist is Samīḥa. In 'al-Qabw' too, while walking through the city the protagonist suddenly remembers 'Samīḥa, the girl who used to love me innocently and genuinely'. Considering that as we have seen, 'al-Qabw' contains a significant autobiographical element, this name perhaps also had a referent in the author's personal life at the time of writing.

16 Tamir, 'al-Badawī', 21.

17 Ibid., 22.

18 Ṣubḥī Ḥadīdī, 'al-Tībūlūjiyā wa al-khaṣā'iṣ al-lughawiyya wa al-uslūbiyya lil-'alāma al-idyūlūjiyya fi qaṣṣ Zakariyyā Tamir (al-badawī namūdhaj[an])' (Typology, linguistic and stylistic peculiarities of the ideological mark in Zakariyyā Tamir's short story – the example of al-badawī), in *Zakariyyā Tamir: masāmīr fi khashab al-tawābīt*, 90–116.

19 Tamir, 'al-Badawī', 52.

20 Stephen Humphrey, 'The Strange Career of Pan-Arabism', in *The Modern Middle East: A Reader*, ed. Albert Hourani, Philip Khoury and Mary C. Wilson (London: I.B. Tauris, 2011), 578–80.

21 Adeed Dawisha, *Arab Nationalism in the Twentieth Century: From Triumph to Despair* (Princeton: Princeton University Press, 2003), 252–82.

22 Patrick Seale, *Asad of Syria: The Struggle for the Middle East* (London: Tauris, 1988), 202.

23 Tamir, *Dimashq al-ḥarā'iq*, 127.

24 Ibid, 134.

25 Frédéric Lagrange, 'Male Homosexuality in Modern Arabic Literature', in *Imagined Masculinities: Male Identity and Culture in the Modern Middle East*, ed. Mai Ghoussoub and Emma Sinclair-Webb (London: Saqi 2000), 169–98.

26 Dalya Cohen-Mor, *Fathers and Sons in the Arab Middle East* (New York: Palgrave Macmillan, 2013), 7.

27 Tamir, *al-Numūr fī al-yawm al-ʿāshir*, 88.
28 Kamal Abu Deeb, 'Cultural Creation in a Fragmented Society', in *The Next Arab Decade – Alternative Futures*, ed. Hisham Sharabi (Boulder and London: Westview/Mansell 1988), 164.
29 This story appeared for the first time in 1976 and was later included in *al-Numūr fī al-yawm al-ʿāshir*. Zakariyyā Tamir, 'Fī layla min al-layālī', *al-Maʿrifa* 168 (February 1976): 82.
30 Aghacy, *Masculine Identity in the Fiction of the Arab East Since 1967*, 95.
31 Ibid., 3.
32 Connell, *Masculinities*, 80.

Chapter 3

1 Certain parts of this chapter are adapted from my article 'Representations of Female Eroticism in Zakariyyā Tamir: The Women's Revolution from Object to Subject', *La Rivista di ArabLit* 10 (2016): 7–27.
2 Pinar Ilkkaracan, 'Sexuality, and Social Change in the Middle East and the Maghreb', *Social Research* 3 (Fall 2002): 753–79.
3 Yvonne Yazbeck Haddad, 'Islam and Gender: Dilemmas in the Changing Arab World', in *Islam, Gender and Social Change*, ed. Yvonne Yazbeck Haddad and John L. Esposito (Oxford: Oxford University Press, 1998), 3.
4 Deniz Kandiyoti, ed., *Gendering the Middle East – Emerging Perspectives* (London: I.B. Tauris, 1996), 9.
5 Sharabi, *Neopatriarchy*, 3–6.
6 Sāra Abū ʿAsalī, ʿal-Ḥaraka al-nisāʾiyya fi sūriyya: min al-ʿawra ilā al-thawra', Available at https://bloggingonsyria.wordpress.com/, on 14 February 2014.
7 Kumari Jayawardena, *Feminism and Nationalism in the Third World* (London: Zed Books, 1992), 2–10.
8 Sara Lei Sparre, 'Educated Women in Syria: Servants of the State, or Nurturers of the Family?', *Critique: Critical Middle Eastern Studies* 17, no. 1 (2008): 3–20.
9 Beth Baron, *Egypt as a Woman – Nationalism, Gender and Politics* (Berkeley: University of California Press, 2005).
10 Wedeen, *Ambiguities of Domination*, 55–6.
11 Abu Deeb, 'The Collapse of the Totalizing Discourse', 344–5.
12 Tamir, *Rabīʿ fī al-Ramād*, 15.
13 Ibid., 14.
14 Tamir, *Ṣahīl al- jawād al-abyaḍ*, 8.

15 Ibid., 104.
16 Ibid., 105.
17 Ibid.
18 Ibid., 106.
19 Zakariyyā Tamir, 'Wajh al-Qamar', *al-Ādāb* 8 (August 1962): 20–1.
20 For a full translation of this story in English, see Husam al-Khateeb, 'A Modern Syrian Short Story', *Journal of Arabic Literature* 3 (1972): 96–105.
21 Ibid., 101.
22 Ibid, 102.
23 Tamir, *Dimashq al-ḥarā'iq*, 312. All excerpts from Tamer, *Tigers on the Tenth Day and Other Stories*, 47–55.
24 Tamer, *Tigers on the Tenth Day and Other Stories*, 48.
25 Ibid., 50.
26 Tamir, *al-Ra'd*, 71.
27 Ibid., 74.
28 'واحدة ما باس تمّها غير أمّها' - wāḥida mā bās timm-ha ġayr umm-ha.
29 Ibid., 79.
30 Kamal Abu Deeb, 'Cultural Creation in a Fragmented Society', in *The Next Arab Decade – Alternative Futures*, ed. Hisham Sharabi (Boulder and London: Westview/Mansell 1988), 166–7.
31 Sharabi, *Neopatriarchy*, 7.
32 Human Rights Watch, *Syria Unmasked – The Suppression of Human Rights by the Asad Regime* (New Haven and London: Yale University Press, 1991), 38–40.
33 Najīb Maḥfūẓ, *Zuqāq al-midaqq* (Cairo: Maktabat Miṣr, 1947).
34 Lagrange, 'Homosexuality in Modern Arabic literature', 177.
35 Ghassān Kanafānī, *Rijāl fī al-shams* (Beirut: Dār ṭalī'a, 1963).
36 Meyer, *The Experimental Arabic Novel*, 27.
37 al-Ṭayyib Ṣāliḥ, *Mawsim al-hijra ila al-shamāl* (Beirut: Dār al-'awda, 1972).
38 Ṭarābīshī, *Sharq wa gharb*, 151.
39 Tamir, *al-Numūr fī al-yawm al-'āshir*, 117–21.
40 Hishām al-Bustānī, 'Rughm al-Ishārāt lā taḥṣul al-taḥawwulāt', *al-Rā'y - al-Malḥaq al-Thaqāfī*, 13 November 2015, http://www.alrai.com/article/749023.html.

Chapter 4

1 Tamir, *Dimashq al-ḥarā'iq*, 11.
2 Tamir, *Sa-naḍḥak*, 120.

3 Maggie Ann Bowers, *Magic(al) Realism* (London and New York: Routledge, 2004), 33–4.

4 Tamir, *Nidā' Nūḥ*, 233.

5 Stephan Guth, 'The Changing Role of Pleasure, or: Towards a Fundamentalist Humanism: Some Thoughts on the Place of Pleasure and Desire in the System of a New Period', in *Desire, Pleasure and the Taboo: New Voices and Freedom of Expression in Modern Arabic Literature*, ed. S. Boustani [et al.] (Pisa & Roma: Fabrizio Serra Editore, 2014), 115–41, 121–3.

6 Ibid., 124.

7 Censi, 'Tra critica sociale ed erotismo', 21–2.

8 Sa'dAllāh Wannūs, *Ṭuqūs al-ishārāt wa al-taḥawwulāt* (Beirut: Dār al-Ādāb, 1994).

9 'أوصانا الرسول بسابع جار' – 'the Prophet instructed us to take care of our neighbours up to seven doors away'.

10 Tamir, *Sa-naḍḥak*, 151.

11 Eric Gautier, 'La femme enviée de Zakariyya Tamir', in *La Syrie au présent: reflets d'une société*, ed. Baudouin Dupret et al. (Arles: Sindbad-Actes Sud, 2010), 515.

12 'My Interview with Zakariyya Tamir', in *Zakariyya Tamir: Storie siriane o storie umane? Un esperimento di traduzione dall'arabo*, ed. Alessandro Columbu (MA dissertation, University of Bologna, 2012), 104.

13 'My Interview with Zakariyya Tamir', 105.

14 Ibid.

15 Zakaria Tamer and Ibrahim Muhawi, trans., *Breaking Knees* (Garnet, 2008), 8.

16 Guth, 'The Changing Role of Pleasure', 124.

17 Tamer, *Breaking Knees*, 13.

18 Tamir, *al-Ḥiṣrim*, 52.

19 Tamer, *Breaking Knees*, 77.

20 Ibid.

21 Wedeen, *Ambiguities of Domination*, 54.

22 Weiss, 'Who Laughs Last', 143.

23 Tamer, *Breaking Knees*, 46.

24 Ibid., 47.

25 Faysal Darraj, 'al-Ru'b wa al-kitāba 'inda Zakariyyā Tamir in Jamāl Shaḥayyid', in *al-Qiṣṣa al-sūrīya fī Sūriyya: aṣālatuhā wa-taqnīyātuhā al-sardiyya: al-awrāq al-muqaddama fī al-nadwa al-mun'aqida takrīman lil-kātibayn 'Abd al-Salām al-'Ujaylī wa Zakariyyā Tāmir* (Damascus: al-Ma'had al-Faransī lil-Sharq al-Awsaṭ (ifpo), Qism al-Dirāsāt al-'Arabiyya, 2004), 19–30.

26 Tamer, *Breaking Knees*, 119.

27 Ibid., 120.
28 *Et Maintenant On Vas Ou? – Wa Halla' La-wayn*. Directed by Nadine Labaki [Film] (Lebanon: Les Films de Tournelles, 2011).
29 Talk at IFPO Damascus. Available at https://archive.org/details/zakariya-tamer-realite-lundis-litteraires-ifpo-5, on 6 September 2014.
30 Tamer, *Breaking Knees*, 75–6.
31 Sabry Hafez, 'Women's Narrative in Modern Arabic Literature', in *Love, Marriage and Sexuality in Modern Arabic Literature*, ed. Roger Allen and Hillary Kilpatrick (London: Saqi Books, 1994), 157.
32 Censi, 'Tra critica sociale ed erotismo', 23.

Chapter 5

1 Certain parts of this chapter are adapted from my article 'Of Knives, Mustaches and Headgears: The Fall of the Qabaday in Zakariyya Tamir's Latest Works' included in the edited volume *Constructions of Masculinities in the Middle East and North Africa: Literature, Film and National Discourse*, ed. Mohja Kahf and Nadine Sinno (The American University in Cairo Press, 2021).
2 Wedeen, *Ambiguities of Domination*, 73–83.
3 Tamer, *Breaking Knees*, 147.
4 Tamir, *Sa-naḍḥak*, 55.
5 Hassan Daoud, 'Those Two Heavy Wings on Manhood: On Moustaches', in *Imagined Masculinities*, ed. Mai Ghoussoub and Emma Sinclair-Webb, 273–80.
6 Tamer, *Breaking Knees*, 114.
7 Ibid., 113.
8 Ibid.
9 Ibid.
10 Aghacy, *Masculine Identity in the Fiction of the Arab East Since 1967*, 183.
11 *The Holy Bible*, Ezekiel, 18:2.
12 Ahmad Daḥbūr, 'Ta'kīd al-qiyam bi-naqīḍiha (qiṣaṣ Zakariyyā Tamir tuṭ'imuna al-ḥiṣrim wa abnā'una yaḍrasuna..!)', in *Zakariyyā Tamir: masāmīr fi khashab al-tawābīt*, 222–3.
13 Ibid., 214–15.
14 Stehli-Werbeck, 'The Poet of the Arabic Short Story', 227.
15 *al-Qur'an*, Yūsuf, 12:5. All Quranic quotations from *The Qur'ān – A New Translation*, trans. M.A.S. Abdel Haleem (Oxford: Oxford University Press, 2005).

16 Tamir, *al-Ḥiṣrim*, 13–18.
17 Ibid., 19–24.
18 Literally 'Alī's mother, using the common Arab paedonymic of referring to a person by the name of their children, but also a popular nickname used in the Syrian vernacular to describe a haughty woman.
19 Tamir, *al-Ḥiṣrim*, 13.
20 Philip Shoukri Khoury, 'Abu Ali al-Kilawi: A Damascus Qabaday', in *Struggle and survival in the Modern Middle East*, ed. Edmund Burke, III and David N. Yaghoubian (Berkeley, Los Angeles, London: University of California Press, 2006), 153–9.
21 'Antara Ibn Shaddād is considered one of the greatest poets of the pre-Islamic period and is the object of tales and legends. Born to a black slave mother he obtained his freedom and fell in love with his cousin 'Abla. For more information about this historical figure, see Griffithes Wheeler Thatcher, "Antara ibn Shaddād', in *Encyclopædia Britannica, 2*, ed. Hugh Chisholm (Cambridge: Cambridge University Press, 1911), 88–9; Touria Khannous, 'Race in Pre-Islamic Poetry: The Work of Antara Ibn Shaddad', *African and Black Diaspora: An International Journal* 6 (2013): 66–80.
22 Tamir, *al-Ḥiṣrim*, 22.
23 Aghacy, *Masculine Identity in the Fiction of the Arab East Since 1967*, 4.
24 Tamir, *al-Ḥiṣrim*, 161.
25 Ibid., 162.
26 John McHugo, *Syria – A Recent History* (London: Saqi Books, 2014), 70–1.
27 Ibid., 67.
28 Philip Shoukri Khouri, *Syria and the French Mandate – The Politics of Arab Nationalism 1920–1945* (Princeton: Princeton University Press, 1987), 73–4.
29 Seale, *Asad of Syria*, 14–16.
30 Tamir, *al-Ḥiṣrim*, 164.
31 Selim Deringil, 'The Invention of Tradition as Public Image in the Late Ottoman Empire, 1808 to 1908', *Comparative Studies in Society and History* 35, no. 1 (January 1993): 9.
32 Zakariyyā Tamir, 'al-Liḥā', *Shi'r* 33, no. 1 (1967): 135–7.
33 Hutcheon argues that irony is 'an interpretative move'. The reader must return to the passage multiple times to 'infer meaning in addition to and different from what is stated, together with an attitude toward both the said and unsaid'. See Linda Hutcheon, *Irony's Edge: The Theory and Politics of Irony* (London: Routledge, 2005), 11.
34 Stehli-Werbeck, 'The Poet of the Arabic Short Story: Zakariyya Tamir', 228.

35 Rebecca Joubin, *The Politics of Love – Sexuality, Gender and Marriage in Syrian Television Drama* (Lanham: Lexington, 2015), 2–8.

36 Ibid., 65.

37 Connell, *Masculinities*, 78.

38 Article 520 of Syria's penal code states: 'Any unnatural sexual intercourse shall be punished with a term of imprisonment of up to three years.'

39 Ghoussoub and Sinclair-Webb, *Imagined Masculinities*, 15.

40 Ṭarābīshī, *Sharq wa gharb*, 5–17.

41 Ibid., 7.

42 Ibid., 78.

43 Ibid.

44 Ṭarābīshī, *Sharq wa gharb*, 15.

45 Lagrange, 'Male Homosexuality in Modern Arabic Literature', 169.

46 Tamer, *Breaking Knees*, 51.

47 Ibid., 50.

48 Ibid., 51.

49 'If virginity is the proof of a women's virtue, what is the proof of men's?' – *Wedding in Galilee*.

50 Tamer, *Breaking Knees*, 91.

51 For more information on the *shabbiha*, see Yasin al-Haj Salih, 'The Syrian Shabiha and Their State: Statehood and Participation', Available at https://lb.boell.org/en/2014/03/03/syrian-shabiha-and-their-state-statehood-participation, on 12 January 2016.

52 Tamer, *Breaking Knees*, 94.

53 Lagrange, 'Male Homosexuality in Modern Arabic Literature', 190.

54 Ṭarābīshī, *Sharq wa gharb*, 5.

Appendix

1 This table is based loosely on the one included in Soraya Botrous's *Les Influences Occidentales sur la nouvelle en Syrie Depuis 1946*, 109–10.

Bibliography

'Abbās, Amīna. 'Ba'da ṣudūr kitābiha *awrāq min sanawāt al-ḥarb 'ala Sūriyya* Nādiā Khūst: kathīr min udabā'ina la 'alāqa lahum bi al-wāqi' wa mu'ẓamuhum ma zāla yugharrid khārij al-sirb', *al-Ba'th*, 4 December 2014. Available at http:/albaath .news.sy/?p=29419, on 05 December 2014.

Abū 'Asalī, Sāra. 'al-Ḥaraka al-nisā'iyya fi sūriyya: min al-'awra ilā al-thawra', Available at https://bloggingonsyria.wordpress.com/, on 14 February 2014.

Accad, Evelyne. *Veil of Shame: The Role of Women in Contemporary Fiction of North Africa and the Arab World*, Québec: Éditions Naaman, 1978.

Aghacy, Samira. *Masculine Identity in the Fiction of the Arab East Since 1967*, Syracuse: Syracuse University Press, 2009.

Allen, Roger. *The Arabic Novel – An Historical and Critical Introduction*, Manchester: The University of Manchester, 1982.

Allen, Roger. 'Literary History and the Arab Novel', *World Literature Today* 2 (Spring 2001): 205–13.

Allen, Roger and Hillary Kilpatrick, eds. *Love, Marriage and Sexuality in Modern Arabic Literature*, London: Saqi Books, 1994.

Badawi, Mustafa M., ed. *Modern Arabic Literature*, Cambridge: Cambridge University Press, 1992.

Badran, Margot and miriam cooke, eds. *Opening the Gates: A Century of Arab Feminist Writing*, London: Virago Press ltd., 1990.

Bahā', Jafra, 'Muthaqqafūn wa fannānūn sūriyyūn ḍidda al-thawra', Available at https://goo.gl/kz287K, on 5 December 2013.

Barakat, Halim. *The Arab World – Society, Culture, and State*, Berkeley: University of California Press, 1993.

Baron, Beth. *Egypt as a Woman - Nationalism, Gender and Politics*, Berkeley: University of California Press, 2005.

Batatu, Hanna. *Syria's Peasantry, the Descendants of its Lesser Rural Notables, and Their Politics*, Princeton: Princeton University Press, 1999.

al-Bayārī, Mu'in. 'Zakariyyā Tamir . . . al-wisām thumma al-hijā'(Zakariyyā Tamir . . . the Decoration, and then the Satire), *Ṣafḥāt sūriyya*, 6 May 2012.

Botrus, Souraya. *Les Influences Occidentales sur la nouvelle en Syrie Depuis 1946*, PhD dissertation, University of Paris-Sorbonne, December 1987.

Boullata, Issa J., ed. *Critical Perspectives on Modern Arabic Literature 1945–1980*, Washington: Three Continents Press, 1980.

Boustani, Soubhi et al. eds. *Desire, Pleasure and the Taboo: New Voices and Freedom of Expression in Modern Arabic Literature*, Pisa & Roma: Fabrizio Serra Editore, 2014.

Bowers, Maggie Ann. *Magic(al) Realism*, London and New York: Routledge, 2004.

Bū 'Alī Yāsīn, *al- Thālūth al-muḥarram – dirāsāt fī al-dīn wa al-jins wa al-ṣirā' al-ṭabaqī*, Beirut: Dār al- Ṭalī'a, 1973.

Burke, III Edmund and David N. Yaghoubian eds. *Struggle and Survival in the Modern Middle East*, Berkeley, Los Angeles, London: University of California Press, 2006.

al-Bustānī, Hishām. 'Rughm al-Ishārāt la taḥṣul al-taḥawwulāt', *al-Rā'y - al-Malḥaq al-Thaqāfī*, 13 November 2015. Available at http://www.alrai.com/article/749023.html, on 13 November 2015.

Camus, Albert. *L'Étranger*, Paris: Gallimard, 1942.

Camus, Albert. *La Peste*, Paris: Gallimard, 1947.

Censi, Martina. 'Tra critica sociale ed erotismo, un esempio della nuova narrativa siriana: Ḥurrās al-hawā' di Rūzā Yāsīn Ḥasan', *La rivista di ArabLit* I, no. 2 (2011): 21–38.

al-Chukr, Dima. 'Interview', *Banipal* 53 (Summer 2015): 114–32.

Cohen-Mor, Dalya. *Fathers and Sons in the Arab Middle East*, New York: Palgrave Macmillan, 2013.

Columbu, Alessandro. *Zakariyya Tamir: Storie siriane o storie umane. Un esperimento di traduzione dall'arabo*, MA Dissertation, University of Bologna, July 2012.

Connell, R. W. *Gender and Power*, Stanford: Stanford University Press, 1987.

Connell, R. W. *Masculinities*, Berkeley: University of California Press, 2005.

Connell, R. W. and Messerschmidt James. 'Hegemonic Masculinity: Rethinking the Concept', *Gender and Society* 19, no. 6 (2005): 829–59.

cooke, miriam. 'Living in Truth', in *Tradition, Modernity and Postmodernity in Arabic Literature – Essays in honour of Professor Issa J. Boullata*, ed. Wael Hallaq and Kamal Abdel-Malek, 203–19. Leiden-Boston-Köln: Brill, 2000.

cooke, miriam. *Dissident Syria* Durham and London: Duke University Press, 2007.

Dawisha, Adeed. *Arab Nationalism in the Twentieth Century: From Triumph to Despair*, Princeton: Princeton University Press, 2003.

Deringil, Selim. 'The Invention of Tradition as Public Image in the Late Ottoman Empire, 1808 to 1908', *Comparative Studies in Society and History* 35, no. 1 (January 1993): 3–29.

Di-Capua, Yoav. 'Arab Existentialism: A Lost Chapter in the Intellectual History of Decolonization', *American Historical Review* 17, no. 4 (October 2012): 1061–91.

Dīb, Kamāl. *Tārīkh Sūriyya al-muʿāṣir – min al-intidāb al-faransī ila ṣayf 2011*, Beirut: Dār al-nahār, 2011.

Dupret, Baudouin et al., eds. *La Syrie au présent: Reflets d'une société*, Arles: Sindbad-Actes Sud, 2010.

Eagleton, Terry. *Marxism and Literary Criticism*, Berkeley and Los Angeles: University of California Press, 1976.

Eagleton, Terry. *Literary Theory – An Introduction*, Oxford: Blackwell Publishing, 1983.

el-Ariss, Tarik. *Trials of Arab Modernity – Literary Affects and the New Political*, New York: Fordham University Press, 2013.

Et Maintenant On Vas Ou? – Wa Halla' La-wayn, Directed by Nadine Labaki [Film]. Lebanon: Les Films de Tournelles.

Firat, Alexa. 'Cultural Battles on the Literary Field: From the Syrian Writers' Collective to the Last Days of Socialist Realism in Syria', *Middle Eastern Literatures* 18, no. 2 (2015): 153–76.

Firat, Alexa and R. Shareah Taleghani, eds. *Generations of Dissent – Intellectuals, Cultural Production, and the State in the Middle East and North Africa*, Syracuse: Syracuse University Press, 2020.

Ghalioun, Bourhan. *La malaise arabe. L'état contre la Nation*, Paris: La Découverte, 1991.

Ghoussoub, Mai and Emma Sinclair-Webb. *Imagined Masculinities: Male Identity and Culture in the Modern Middle East*, London: Saqi 2000.

Haddad, Yvonne Yazbeck and L. Esposito John, eds. *Islam Gender and Social Change*, Oxford: Oxford University Press, 1998.

Ḥadīdī, Ṣubḥī. 'Poet of the Short Story', *Banipal* 53 (Summer 2015): 74–7.

Hafiz, Sabry. *The Quest for Identities – The Development of the Modern Arabic Short Story*, London: Saqi Books, 2007.

Hafiz, Sabry and Cobham Catherine, eds. *A Reader of Modern Arabic Short Stories*, London: Saqi Books, 1988.

al-Haj Salih, Yasin. 'The Syrian Shabiha and Their State: Statehood and Participation', Available at https://lb.boell.org/en/2014/03/03/syrian-shabiha-and-their-state-statehood-participation, on 3 March 2014.

Hallaq, Wael and Kamal Abdel-Malek, eds. *Tradition, Modernity and Postmodernity in Arabic Literature – Essays in Honour of Professor Issa J. Boullata*, Leiden-Boston-Köln: Brill, 2000.

Hanna, Kifah. *Feminism and Avant-Garde Aesthetics in the Levantine Novel*, New York: Palgrave MacMillian, 2016.

Harlow, Barbara. *Resistance Literature*, New York: Methuen, 1987.

Hourani, Albert, Khoury Philip and Mary C. Wilson, eds. *The Modern Middle East: A Reader*, London: I. B. Tauris, 2011.

Human Rights Watch, *Syria Unmasked - The Suppression of Human Rights by the Asad Regime*, New Haven and London: Yale University Press, 1991.

Ḥusayn, Haytham. 'Istīṭān al-khawf: al-muthaqqaf al-'arabī al-madh'ūr' (Settling Fear: The Paranoid Arab Intellectual), *al-'Arab*, 08 June 2014.

Ḥusayn, Ṭāhā, 'al-Adīb yaktubu lil-khāṣṣa', *al-Ādāb*, 5 (May 1955): 9–16.

Husni, Ronak and L. Newman Daniel. *Modern Arabic Short Stories: A Bilingual Reader*, London: Saqi Books, 2012.

Hutcheon, Linda. *Irony's Edge: The Theory and Politics of Irony*, London: Routledge, 2005.

Ibrāhīm, Ṣun'Allāh. *Tilka al-rā'iḥa*, Cairo: Maktabat Yūliyū, 1966.

'Īd, 'Abd al-Razzāq. *al-'Ālam al-qiṣaṣī li-Zakariyyā Tamir*, Beirut: Dār al-fārābī, 1989.

Ilkkaracan, Pinar. 'Sexuality, and Social Change in the Middle East and the Maghreb', *Social Research* 3 (Fall 2002): 753–79.

Jarād, Ibrāhim, ed. *Zakariyyā Tamir: masāmīr fi khashab al-tawābīt*, Damascus: Ittiḥād al-Kuttāb al-'Arab, 2011.

Jayawardena, Kumari. *Feminism and Nationalism in the Third World*, London: Zed Books, 1992.

Johnson-Davis, Denys trans. *Arabic Short Stories*, Los Angeles and Berkeley: University of California Press, 1983.

Joubin, Rebecca. *The Politics of Love – Sexuality, Gender and Marriage in Syrian Television Drama*, Lanham: Lexington, 2015.

Joubin, Rebecca. 'The Politics of the Qabaday (tough man) and the Changing Father Figure in Syrian Television Drama', *Journal of Middle East Women's Studies* 12, no. 1 (2016): 50–67.

Joubin, Rebecca. *Mediating the Uprising: Narratives of Gender and Marriage in Syrian Television Drama*, New Brunswick: Rutgers University Press, 2020.

Kahf, Mohja. 'The Silences of Contemporary Syrian Literature', *World Literature Today* 75, no. 2 (2001): 224–36.

Kanafānī, Ghassān. *Rijāl fī al-shams*, Beirut: Dār ṭalī'a, 1963.

Kanafānī, Ghassān. *Adab al-muqāwama fī Filasṭīn al-muḥtalla 1948-1966*, Beirut: Dār al-Ādāb, 1966.

Kandiyoti, Deniz, ed. *Gendering the Middle East – Emerging Perspectives*, London: I. B. Tauris, 1996.

al-Kawākibī, 'Abd al-Raḥman. *al-A'māl al-kāmila lil-Kawākibī*, Beirut: Markaz dirāsāt al-waḥda al-'arabiyya, 1995.

Kayyal, Mahmoud. 'Damascene Shahrazad – The Images of Women in Zakariyya Tamir's Stories', *Hawwa* 4 (2006): 93–113, 189–91.

Kedar, Mordechai. *Asad in Search of Legitimacy – Message and Rhetoric in the Syrian Press under Hafiz and Bashar*, Brighton: Sussex Academic Press, 2005.

Keddie, Nikki R. *Women in the Middle East – Past and Present*, Princeton: Princeton University Press, 2007.

Kepel, Gilles et Richard, Yann, eds. *Intellectuels et Militants de l'Islam Contemporain*, Paris: Seuil, 1990.

Khalīfa, Khālid. *Madīḥ al-Karāhīya*, Damascus: Dār Amīsa, 2006.

Khalīfa, Muṣṭafā. *al-Qawqa'*, Beirut: Dar al-Ādāb, 2008.

Khannous, Touria. 'Race in pre-Islamic Poetry: The Work of Antara Ibn Shaddad', *African and Black Diaspora: An International Journal* 6 (2013): 66–80.

al-Khateeb, Husam. 'A Modern Syrian Short Story', *The Journal of Arabic Literature* 3 (1972): 96–105.

al-Khaṭīb, Muḥammad Kāmil. *'Ālam Ḥannā Mīna al-riwā'ī*, Beirut: Dār al-ādāb, 1979.

al-Khaṭīb, Muḥammad Kāmil, Nabīl Sulaymān and Bū 'Alī Yāsīn, eds. *Ma'ārik thaqāfiyya fī Sūriyya 1975-1977*, Beirut: Dār ibn Rushd, 1978.

Khouri, Philip Shoukri. *Syria and the French Mandate – The Politics of Arab Nationalism 1920–1945*, Princeton: Princeton University Press, 1987.

Klemm, Verena. 'Different Notions of Commitment (iltizam) and Committed Literature (al-adab al-multazim) in the Literary Circles of the Mashriq', *Arabic and Middle Eastern Literature* 3, no. 1 (2000): 51–62.

Lei Sparre, Sara. 'Educated Women in Syria: Servants of the State, or Nurturers of the Family?', *Critique: Critical Middle Eastern Studies* 17, no. 1 (2008): 3–20.

Lesch, David W. *The New Lion of Damascus – Bashar al-Asad and Modern Syria*, New Haven and London: Yale University Press, 2005.

M.A.S. Abdel Haleem, trans. *The Qur'ān – A New Translation*, Oxford: Oxford University Press, 2005.

Maḥfūẓ, Najīb. *Zuqāq al-midaqq*, Cairo: Maktabat Misr, 1947.

Majed, Ziad. 'A Dialogue with Zakaria Tamer', Available at https://goo.gl/TfmkAf, *on* 5 June 2012.

Massad, Joseph. 'Conceiving the Masculine: Gender and Palestinian Nationalism', *Middle East Journal* 3 (Summer 1995): 467–83.

Massad, Joseph. *Desiring Arabs*, Chicago: The University of Chicago Press, 2007.

McHugo, John. *Syria – A Recent History*, London: Saqi Books, 2014.

Mernissi, Fatima. *Beyond the Veil – Male-female Dynamics in Modern Muslim Societies*, Revised edition, Bloomington and Indianapolis: Indiana University Press, 1987.

Meyer, Stefan G. *The Experimental Arabic Novel – Postcolonial Literary Modernism in the Levant*, New York: State University of New York Press, 2001.

Mīna, Ḥannā. 'Fi al-tajriba al-riwā'iyya', *al-Ma'rifa* 224 (October 1980).

Mīna, Ḥannā. *al-Maṣābīḥ al-zurq*, Beirut: Dār al-Ādāb, 1989. 1st edition, Beirut: Dār al-Fikr al-Jadīd, 1954.

Moubayed, Sami M. *Steel & Silk: Men and Women who Shaped Syria 1900–2000* Seattle: Cune Press, 2005.

Neep, Daniel. *Occupying Syria under the French Mandate*, Cambridge: Cambridge University Press, 2012.

Neuwirth, Angelika, Andreas Pflitsch and Barbara Winckler, eds. *Arabic Literature: Postmodern Perspectives*, London: Saqi Books, 2010.

Nice, Pamela. 'Finding the Right Language: A Conversation with Syrian filmmaker Usama Muhammad', *Al-jadid: A Review and Record of Arab Culture and Arts* 6, no. 31 (Spring 2000).

O'Connor, Frank. *The Lonely Voice - A Study of the Short Story*, London: Macmillan and Co., 1963.

Pannewick, Frederick and Georges Khalil, eds. *Commitment and Beyond – Reflections on/of the Political in Arabic Literature since the 1940s*, Wiesbaden: Reichert Verlag 2015.

Qaddūr, 'Umar. 'al-Riwāya al-Sūriyya al-Jadīda: ẓāhira ibdā'iyya am ẓāhira i'lāmiyya?', *al-Ādāb* 9–10 (2009): 98–101.

al-Qaḍmānī, Riḍwān. *Zakariyyā Tamir: mu'jaz al-qaswa wa al-ra'b*, Damascus: al-Amāna al-'āmma li-iḥtifāliyyat Dimashq 'āṣimat al-thaqāfa al-'arabiyya, 2008.

Ruocco, Monica. *L'intellettuale arabo tra impegno e dissenso – Analisi della rivista libanese al-Ādāb (1953–1994)*, Rome: Jouvence, 1999.

Ṣadiq, Mīrfāt. 'Jā'iza Maḥmūd Darwīsh li- Zakariyyā Tamir wa Hāni Abū As'ad', *al-Jazīra*, 15 March 2015. Available at https://goo.gl/PxcPkZ, on March 2015.

Said, Edward W. *Reflections on Exile and Other Literary and Cultural Essays*, London: Granta Books, 2001.

Salti, Rasha. *Insights into Syrian Cinema*, New York: Rattapallax Press, 2006.

al-Ṣamādī, Imtinān 'Uthmān. *Zakariyyā Tamir wa al-qiṣṣa al-qaṣīra*, 'Ammān: Wizārat al-Thaqāfa, 1995.

Sartre, Jean-Paul. *Qu'est-ce que la littérature?* Paris: Gallimard, 1948.

Seale, Patrick. *Asad of Syria – The Struggle for the Middle East*, London: I.B. Tauris, 1988.

Shaḥayyid, Jamāl. *al-Qiṣṣa al-sūrīya fī Sūriyya: aṣālatuhā wa-taqnīyātuhā al-sardiyya: al-awrāq al-muqaddama fī al-nadwa al-mun'aqida takrīman lil-kātibayn 'Abd al-Salām al- 'Ujaylī wa Zakariyyā Tāmir*, Damascus: al-Ma'had al-Faransī lil-Sharq al-Awsaṭ (ifpo), Qism al-Dirāsāt al-'Arabiyya, 2004.

Shaheen, Mohammad. *The Modern Arabic Short Story – Shahrazad Returns*, London: Macmillan Press, 1989.

Sharabi, Hisham. *Neopatriarchy – A Theory of Distorted Change in Arab Society*, Oxford: Oxford University Press 1988.

Sharabi, Hisham, ed. *The Next Arab Decade – Alternative Futures*, Boulder and London: Westview/Mansell 1988.

Starkey, Paul. *Modern Arabic Literature*, Edinburgh: Edinburgh University Press, 2006.

Starkey, Paul. *Sonallah Ibrahim – Rebel with a Pen*, Edinburgh: Edinburgh University Press, 2016.

Stephan, Rita. 'Arab Women Writing Their Sexuality', *Hawwa* 4, no. 2 (2006): 159–80.

Ṣubḥī, Muḥyī al-dīn. 'Muqābala ma' Zakariyyā Tamir' (Interview with Zakariyyā Tamir), *al-Ma'rifa*, 126 (August 1972).

Sulaymān, Nabīl and Bū 'Alī Yāsīn. *al-Adab wa al-idıyūlūjıyā fī Sūriyya 1967–1973*, Beirut: Dār Ibn Khaldūn, 1974.

Taleghani, R. Shareah. 'Vulnerability and Recognition in Syrian Prison Literature', *International Journal of Middle East Studies* 49 (2017): 91–109.

Tamer, Zakaria and Ibrahim Muhawi, trans. *Breaking Knees*, Garnet, 2008.

Tamer, Zakaria. *Tigers on the Tenth Day and Other Stories*, trans. Denys Johnson-Davies, London, Melbourne and New York: Quartet Books, 1985.

Tamir, Zakariyyā. 'al-Qabw', *al-Thaqāfa* 2 (1958): 48.

Tamir, Zakariyyā. 'Raḥīl ila al-baḥr', *al-Ādāb* 11 (November 1960): 18.

Tamir, Zakariyyā. *Ṣahīl al-jawād al-abyaḍ*, Beirut: Dār majallat al-Shi'r, 1960.

Tamir, Zakariyyā. 'al-Badawī', *al-Ādāb* 10 (1962): 21–4, 52–6.

Tamir, Zakariyyā. 'Wajh al-Qamar', *al-Ādāb* 8 (August 1962): 20–1.

Tamir, Zakariyyā. *Rabī' fī al-ramād*, Damascus: Wizārat al-Thaqāfa, 1963.

Tamir, Zakariyyā. 'al-Ṣaqar', *al-Ma'rifa* 75 (May 1968): 43–6.

Tamir, Zakariyyā. *al-Ra'd*, Damascus: Ittiḥād al-kuttāb al-'arab, 1970.

Tamir, Zakariyyā. *Dimashq al-ḥarā'iq*, Damascus: Ittiḥād al-kuttāb al-'arab, 1973.

Tamir, Zakariyyā. 'Ḥaky al-Udabā' al-Aṣfār', *al-Ba'ath*, 7 July 1975.

Tamir, Zakariyyā. 'Fi Layla min al-layālī', *al-Ma'rifa* 168 (February 1976): 82.

Tamir, Zakariyyā. *al-Numūr fī al-yawm al-'āshir*, Beirut: Dār al-Ādāb, 1978.

Tamir, Zakariyyā. 'Qirā'āt', *al-Ma'rifa* 219 (May 1980): 5.

Tamir, Zakariyyā. 'Laysa bi-wazīr wa-lā bi-shā'ir', *al-Taḍāmun* 232 (1987): 66.

Tamir, Zakariyyā. *Nidā' Nūḥ*, London: Riyad el-Rayyes Books, 1994.

Tamir, Zakariyyā. *Sa-naḍḥak*, London: Riyad el-Rayyes Books, 1998.

Tamir, Zakariyyā. *al-Ḥiṣrim*, London: Riyad el-Rayyes Books, 2000.

Tamir, Zakariyyā. *Taksīr rukab*, London: Riyad el-Rayyes Books, 2002.

Tamir, Zakariyyā. *Hijā' al-qatīl li-qātilihi*, Beirut: Riyad el-Rayyes Books, 2003.

Tamir, Zakariyyā. *al-Qunfudh*, London: Riyad el-Rayyes Books, 2005.

Tamir, Zakariyyā. *Arḍ al-wayl*, Beirut: Jadāwil, 2015.

Tarabishi, Georges. *Woman against her Sex – A Critique of Nawal el-Saadawi*, London: Saqi, 1998.

Ṭarābīshī, Jūrj. *al-Adab min al-dākhil*, Beirut: Dār al-ṭalī'a, 1977.

Ṭarābīshī, Jūrj. *Sharq wa gharb: rujūla wa unūtha dirāsa fī azmat al-jins wa al- ḥaḍāra fī al-riwāya al-'arabiyya*, Beirut: Dar al-Talī'a, 1977.

Thatcher, Griffithes Wheeler. 'Antara ibn Shaddād', in *Encyclopædia Britannica, 2*, ed. Hugh Chisholm, Cambridge: Cambridge University Press, 1911.

Tierney-Tello, Mary Beth. *Allegories of Transgression and Transformation: Experimental Fiction by Women Writing under Dictatorship*, Albany: State University of New York Press, 1996.

Trombetta, Lorenzo. *Siria. Dagli Ottomani agli Asad. E oltre*, Milano: Mondadori, 2013.

Vladislav, Jan, ed. *Living in Truth*, London and Boston: Faber and Faber, 1986.

Wannūs, Sa'dallāh. *Ṭuqūs al-ishārāt wa al-taḥawwulāt*, Beirut: Dār al-Ādāb, 1994.

Wedeen, Lisa. *Ambiguities of Domination: Politics, Rhetoric, and Symbols in Contemporary Syria*, Chicago: University of Chicago Press, 1999.

Weiss, Max. 'Who Laughs Last', in *Middle East Authoritarianisms – Governance, Contestation and Resilience in Syria and Iran*, ed. Steven Heydemann and Reinoud Leenders, 143–66, Stanford: Stanford University Press, 2013.

Westney, Emma. 'Individuation and Literature: Zakariyya Tamir and his Café Man', in *Marginal Voices in Literature and Society: Individual and Society in the Mediterranean Muslim World*, dir. Robin Ostle, 189–99, Strasbourg: European Science Foundation (ESF), in collaboration with the Maison Méditerranéenne des Sciences de l'Homme d'Aix-en-Provence, 2000.

Williams, Raymond. *Marxism and Literature*, Oxford: Oxford University Press, 1977.

Yazbik, Samar. *Taqāṭu' nīrān*, Beirut: Dār al-Ādāb, 2012.

Yazbik, Samar. *Bawwābāt arḍ al-'adam*, Beirut: Dār al-Ādāb, 2015.

Ziter, Edward. *Political Performance in Syria – From the Six-Day War to the Syrian Uprising*, New York: Palgrave Macmillan, 2015.

Index

Note: Page numbers followed by 'n' refer notes

Bashār's election and authoritarian legacy 33
conservative and patriarchal Islamism 31
-cum-patriarchy 9
Hama massacre 31
Lebanese civil war in 1975 30–1
new Syrian literature 31–2
opposition to 31
ostracism of Tamir 30
plurality of voices and styles 32
power and politics in Syria 32–3
satirical article 32
struggle against 30–4
surveillance and censorship in Syria 31
authoritarian regime 4, 8, 23, 29, 31, 36, 49, 54, 56, 77, 99, 112
authoritarian state
denouncing of gendered oppression 53–6
al-Numūr fī al-yawm al-ʿāshir 54, 58
feminization as a form of humiliation 56
Fī layla min al-layālī (One night) 54–5
process of interplay of gender 56
transformations of male protagonist 54
objectification of female body 73–6
1963, Emergency Law 74
al-Ightiyal 74–6
domesticated societies 74
Fī layla min al-layālī (One night) 74
indications of male homosexuality 74
military authoritarianism 73
mukhābarāt 74
use of bodily metaphors 74
authorization, concepts of 10
avant-garde aesthetics 15, 117–18
awards received by Tamir
Blue Metropolis Literary Prize 32
Cairo First Short Story Prize in 2009 32
Mahmoud Darwish Award for Freedom and Creativity 32
Sultan Bin Ali Al Owais Cultural Foundation's prize for Stories, Novels and Drama in 2001 32
Syrian Order of Merit in 2002 32, 36
Awwād, Tawfīq Yūsuf 19

Baath party 49, 60, 73
Baghdadi, Shawqi 21
Bakdash, Khalid 18
al-Baqqār, Najīb Bey 104, 106
Barakat, Halim 9
Batatu, Hanna 42
battle of Maysalun 107–8
beys (*beyk* in Arabic) 105
bodily metaphors 74
book of Genesis 23–4, 28

civil war in Lebanon 12, 28, 30, 49, 93
colonization 74, 107
Columbu, Alessandro 126
committed literature (*al-adab al-multazim*) 17
Connell, R.W. 8–9, 119
consciousness 2, 19, 48, 64, 105, 118

Daoud, Hasan 101
death and poverty, connection between 48
Deeb, Kamal Abu 2–3, 40, 57, 79
desire for change 42–3
Dimashq al-harāʾiq (Damascus of fires) 4, 6
domesticated societies 74
dominant role of woman 112–13, *see also* women
Dostoevsky 16

el-Saadawi, Nawal 10–11
emancipation 4, 12, 16, 39, 41, 46, 52–3, 60, 63, 66, 68, 76, 84, 91, 103, 117, 119
Emergency Law of 1963 74
existentialism 15, 20, 45

Farzat, Ali 35
female
body and sexual charge 45–6
-centred writing 84
characters in struggle against patriarchy 61–3

eroticism representations 65
exclusion from decision-making process 72
feminism and gender equality 60
neo-patriarchy and (*see* neo-patriarchy and role of female)
oppressive fathers 62
power and sexual blackmail 93–4
self-confident nature 88
struggles of the marginalized sectors 61–2
Thalj ākhir al-layl (Snow late at night) 62–3
female point of view 66–71
Imr'a wahīda (A lonely woman) 66, 69–70
narratives of modernization 71
and postmodern short story 83–4
exile collection *Nidā Nūḥ* 83
fragmentation of the text 83
new fashion of cultural production 84
Shahriyār and Shahrazād 83
stylistic transformations 83
repression of sexual desire 66
subject/object reversal 67–8
Wajh al-qamar (The moon's face) 66–8, 70
female sexuality and sexual desire 63–6
Al-Ra'd 71
al-Ughniya al-zarqā' al-khashina 63–6
al-'Urs al-sharqī (the Oriental wedding) 71–3
as critique of patriarchal family 71–3
and eroticism 87
exclusion of girl from decision-making process 72
isolation and disenfranchisement of the protagonists 64
objectification of the woman 63
Qaranfula lil-asfalt al-mut'ab (Carnation for the tired tar) 65
representations of 87
sexuality as *fitna*, Mernissi's analysis of 10–11
social issues and male domination 63–4
in stories, published between 1994 and 2002 79
feminine and masculine identities 5
fiction
gender-motivated 11, 84
influence of socialist realism 27
Lebanese fiction writing, post-war period 11–12
and politics 7
prose fiction 27
Fī layla min al-layālī (One night) 53–4, 74, 100
fitna 10–11, 93
Freudianism 20

gender and power in Syrian families 50
gendered oppression, *see* authoritarian state; oppression and gender roles
gender equality 60, 119
gender hierarchy 109
gender-motivated fiction 11, 84
Gouraud, General Henri 107
Gramsci 8
Guth, Stephen 83, 87

Ḥadātha, 1960s and 1970s
al-Bustān
elements of magical realism 80–1
violence and abuses 81
al-Nūmur fī al-yawm al-'āshir 54, 58
authoritarian state and gendered oppression 53–6
as destruction of old order 40–2
freedom from corrupt regimes 41
male's individual and collective emancipation 41
Rabī' fī al-ramād (Spring in the ashes) 40–1
struggle for power 42
Syria's peasantry 42
transformation to secular, emancipatory and nationalist 40–2
Fī layla min al-layālī (One night) 54–5
ḥadāthī thought and literature 57–8
masculinity and patriarchy, representations 57
oppression, gendered dimension 53–6
as quest for purification 42–4

al-Jārima (The crime) 43
desire for change 42–3
patriarchal traditions and institutions 44
pessimistic depictions 43
Raḥīl ila al-bahr (Exodus to the sea) 42–3
stories, influence of the optimism and fervour 42
as revolt against patriarchy and exploitation 44–9
al-Badawī 46–8
al-Qabw (The basement) 44–5
connection between death and poverty 48
disparity in male and female 46
female body and sexual charge 45–6
influences of surrealism and existentialism 45
patriarchy and authoritarianism 52
symbol of poverty and disenfranchisement 45
victimized children 53
Sa-naḍḥak
assertive role of female characters 82
attack on masculinity and honour 81
magical realism 82
ḥadāthī 3, 40, 57–8, 119, *see also* female sexuality and sexual desire; *Ḥ*adātha, 1960s and 1970s
Hafez, Sabry 21, 136 n.4, 148 n.31
Hama massacre 31
al-Hamīd, ʻAbd 112
Ḥaqqī, Yaḥyā 19
Ḥasan, Rūzā Yāsin 31, 84
Ḥaydar, Ḥaydar 34
hegemonic masculinity, concept of 8
Hijā al-qatīl li-qātilihi (*The victim's satire of his killer)* 32
homosexuality 99
homosexual relationships 51
as the sign of decay
dominant role of woman 112–14
gender hierarchy 109
Ḥamlat Nabulyūn (Napoleon's expedition) 110
hypocrisy 112
the invisible desire 114
power relations 109–10
relationship between colonial powers and victims 110
same sex relations 110–11
al-Ḥūrāniyya, Saʻīd 19
Ḥusayn, Ṭāhā 24
hypocrisy 89–90
of patriarchal family 89, 111–12
political 115
religious 41, 66, 70–1, 86
repository of 53

Ibn Shaddād, Antara 105–6, 108, 149 n.21
ideological fragmentation 1–2, 27–9, 57, 84, 96
classics having translations 28–9
cultural production and 86
despotism 29
and female-oriented writing 96
fragmented nature of the text 28
interpretations 28–9
modernism 28
series of sub-stories and sub-paragraphs 28
Idrīs, Suhayl 17, 20
Idrīs, Yūsuf 19
Imra'a jamīla (A beautiful woman) 94
Imra'a wahīda (A lonely woman) 66, 69–70, 75–6, *see also* female point of view
Isbir, Abīr 31

Joubin, Rebecca 109

Kafka 16
Kafkaesque rebellion 43
Kāmil al-Khaṭīb, Muhammad 21–2
Kanafānī, Ghāssan 74
Khaḍrā' al-Jayyūsī, Salma 16
al-Khāl, Yūsuf 16
Khalīfa, Khālid 31
al-Khateeb, Husam 67
Khoury, Philip Shoukri 104
Khūst, Nādyā 34, 111

Labaki, Nadine 93–4
Lāyalī Ibn Āwa (Nights of the Jackals) 112
League of Nations 107

Lebanese civil war, *see* civil war in Lebanon
Lebanese Riyad el-Rayyes Books 32
Les Temps Modernes 20
liberalization of Syrian society 90
literary commitment 1, 16–17, 20, 24, 117
Literature and ideology in Syria 1967–1973 22, 26
Lysistrata (Aristophanes) 94

Ma'ārik thaqāfiyya fī Sūriyya 1975–1977 (Cultural battles in Syria 1975–1977) 22
Madīh al-Karāhiya (In praise of hatred) 32
magical realism 80, 82
Mahmud II, Sultan 108
marginalization 10, 12, 61–2, 75
masculinity
  decline of 100–3
    al-Mutanakkir (the disguised) 101
    collapse of male protagonist's supremacy 100
    disintegration and loss of subjectivity 115
    display of manhood 101–2
    examples 101
    Fī layla min al-layālī 100
    incapacity to women's demands 102
    masculinity and feminization of male characters 115
    oppressor/victim relationship 100
    political hypocrisy 115
    self-enforcing strategies of domination 101
    themes of arbitrary arrest and violence 100–1
    woman's superiority 102–3
  and patriarchy, representations 57
  in stories of 1970s 49–53
    act of parricide 51
    al-'Āila (The family) 51–2
    attitude towards women in Rabī' fī al-ramād 51
    denunciation of alienation and privileges 50
    gender and power in Syrian families 50
    male vulnerability and weakness 51
    multiplicity of voices and themes 49
    Pan-Arab ideology 49
    Tishrīn 49
Mason, James 16
Massad, Joseph 39
Mernissi, Fatima 10–11, 138 n.32
migration 74
military authoritarianism, consolidation of 73
Mīna, Ḥānnā 21, 34
modernization 1–2, 4, 7, 9, 12, 39, 41, 60, 71, 73, 112, 119
Muḥammad, Aḥmad 21
mukhābarāt 73–5
multiplicity 6, 28, 49

Najīb Maḥfūẓ 74, 104, 106
nakba 'the catastrophe' 17
National Cinema Organisation of Syria 112
nationalism 13, 17, 32, 39, 41, 57, 61, 99, 107
national liberation 4, 7, 25, 39, 119
neopatriarchal authoritarianism 114
neo-patriarchy and role of female 59–61
  al-Ḥaraka al-Niswiyya (Women's movement) 60
  association between Palestine and the female body 61
  emancipation and equality 60
  feminism and gender equality 60
  male-centred nature in Tamir's works 61
  modernizing in Syria 60
  participation of women in public sphere 60
Nidā' Nūḥ (Noah's summon) 5, 7, 32, 83, 87, 119
objectification of female characters 57, 63–4, 73–7, 81, 91, 95, 97, 117

O'Connor, Frank 19–21
"One Night," story from *al-Nūmur fī al-yawm al-'āshir* 126–35
One Thousand and One Nights 41
oppression and gender roles 80–2
  al-Bustān
    elements of magical realism 80–1
    violence and abuses 81

Sa-naḍḥak
assertive role of female characters 82
attack on masculinity and honour 81
magical realism 82
oppressive fathers 62
ostracism 30, 36
Ottoman Empire 108

Palestine and the female body, association between 61
Palestinian Darwish foundation 32
Palestinian resistance movement 27
Pan-Arab nationalism 49, 73, 107
patriarchy 5, 9–10, 12, 47–8, 53, 58, 99, *see also* neo-patriarchy and role of female
and authoritarian nationalist discourse 39, 52
female characters in struggle against 62–3
female sexuality and sexual desire as critique 71–3
and gender roles 39–40
hypocrisy of 89–90
organization of 10
revolt against exploitation and 44–9
system 119
traditions and institutions 44
patriotism 25
Peloponnesian war 94
political activism 35, 95, 109, 114–15
pre- and post-1967 writings, chronological demarcation 6

qabaḍay *103–9*
al-Ḥiṣrim 103–4
al-Liḥā (The beards) 108
al-Muṭarbash 106–7
al-Qawīq 104
beys (*beyk* in Arabic), authority of the local notables 104–5
Bilād al-Shām, countries of Greater Syria 107
equal gender relations 109
gender role transformations 106
inequality and class segregation 106
model of delusional masculinity 108
political significance in Syrian culture 108–9
qabaḍay model of masculinity 104–5
symbolic value of the fez 108
symbols of masculinity 104
Qaranfula lil-asfalt al-mut'ab (Carnation for the tired tar) 16, 65, *see also* female sexuality and sexual desire

Rabī' fī al-ramād (Spring in the ashes) 4, 6, 12, 22, 40–1
Raḥīl ilā al-baḥr (Exodus to the sea) 42–3
Rijāl fī al-shams (Men in the sun) 74

Ṣahīl al-jawād al-abyaḍ (The neighing of the White Steed) 4, 6, 16, 22, 44, 61, 63
Sa'īd, Muṣṭafā 74–5
al-Salām al-'Ujaylī, Abd 19
Ṣālih, al-Ṭayyib 74
same-sex relationship 51, 110–11, 113–14, 120
Sāmī al-Jundī 16
Sa-naḍḥak (We shall laugh) 5, 7, 32, 80–4, 87, 101, 119, *see also* oppression and gender roles
assertive role of female characters 82
attack on masculinity and honour 81
magical realism 82
al-Sarrāj, Manhal 31
Sartre, Jean-Paul 16, 20, 24, 39
Sartrean agenda 39
Seale, Patrick 49
Second World War 21
self-empowerment 86
sex and marriage in *al-Ḥisrim* and *Taksīr Rukab*, *see al-Ḥisrim* and *Taksīr Rukab*
sex and politics in *Taksīr Rukab*, *see Taksīr Rukab*
sexuality, *see also* female sexuality and sexual desire
and authoritarianism 121
and gender roles 118
sexual desire, repression of 66
shabbīḥa, Syrian regime thugs 113
Shaddād, Antara Ibn 105, 108, 149 n.21
Sharabi, Hisham 9

al-Shāyb, Fu'ād 19
Six Days War 6
socialism 3, 32, 61, 73
socialist realism and commitment 20–7
  anarchy 26
  autobiographical connotations 21
  book of Genesis 23–4
  committed and tendentious art, distinction 24
  controversy and Tamir's work 22
  excerpt from Alladhī ahraqa al-sufun 23
  Freudianism 20
  individual and society, conflict between 22–3
  literary commitment by Ḥusayn 24–5
  nihilism and uncommitted style 23
  O'Connor's short story and genre's ideology 21
  protagonists' individualism 20
  Rabī' fī al-ramād 22–3
  Russian socialist realism 21
  short story and the novel in Marxist terms 21
  struggle against dominance of petty bourgeoisie 24
  symbolism 20
  Tamir's interview with *al-Ma'rifa* 25–6
Stehli-Werbeck, Ulrike 108
study of contemporary Arabic and Syrian literature 1
subject/object reversal 67–8
Sulaymān, Nabīl 22, 26–7
surrealism 45
Syria and Arab East 1948–78 16–19
  al-ādāb's trajectory 17
  Arab cultural heritage (*al-turāth*) 17
  Arab Writers' Association 18
  ideals of Khālid Bakdāsh 18
  political upheaval in Syria 18
  role of literature and intellectuals 16
  struggle for emancipation of the Arab nation 16
  Syrian Communist Party 17
  Syrian Writers' Collective 17
  trends in cultural production 17
Syria(n)
  Arab Kingdom 108
  authoritarianism 99
  Communist Party 17
  cultures and ethnicities 92–3
  literature and cultural production 136 n.3
  peasantry 42
  political vocabulary 49
  uprising 15
Syrian Ministry of Culture and National Guidance 30
Syrian Muslim Brotherhood 31
Syrian revolution 34–6
  accounts of horrors of Syria's prisons 35
  al-Mihmāz, Facebook page by Tamir 35
  anti-regime portrayals in films and plays 34
  artists refusal to uprising 34
  propagation of digital literature 36
  study of Syrian political language and domination 36
  Tamir's participation in the uprising 35
Syrian Writers' Collective 17, 20

taboo-breaking nature of stories 91–2, 96–7
Taksīr Rukab 33–4, 85, 120, *see also* transgressive female sexuality
  sex and politics in 92–5
    cultures and ethnicities of Syria 92–3
    female body as allegory of nation 94–5
    female power and sexual blackmail 93–4
    Imra'a jamīla (A beautiful woman) 94
    sex as a form of *fitna* 93
    Taksīr Rukab, conceptualization of female power 95
    women as repository of common sense 93–4
Tamerlane, Mongol conqueror 108
Tamir, Zakariyya career and innovation, *see also* awards received by Tamir
  al-Mihmāz, Facebook page 35
  Arab Writers' Union 18

as editor-in-chief of *al-Ma'rifa* 30
first five collections, 1960 and 1978 4
first short stories in late 1950's 16
individualist orientation 19–20
interview with *al-Ma'rifa* 25
literary strategies 4
male-centred nature in works 61
Marxist dimension 2
new techniques and themes 19
photographic style of writing 19
protagonists of Tamir's stories 2
Qaranfula lil-asfalt al-mut'ab (A carnation for the tired tar) 16
Rabī' fī al-ramād 15
relocation to UK and journalistic activities 1, 32
rise of existentialism 20
Syrian contemporary literature, impact of 19
use of bodily and sexual connotations 2
Ṭarābīshī 39, 110, 114
Thalj akhir al-layl (Snow late at night) 16, 62–3, *see also* female
theory of masculinity, Connell's 8–9
Tishrīn 49
transgressive female sexuality
effects of authoritarianism 87
female sexuality and eroticism 87
identities 10, 96
in *al-Ḥisrim* and *Taksīr Rukab* 86–8
portrayals of female characters 118
representations of female sexuality 87
self-confident nature of the female 88
Translation and Publication Department of the Syrian Ministry of Culture (1960–3) 15
Tūqus al-ishārāt wa al-taḥawwulāt (Rituals of signs and transformations, Wannus) 84–5

Wajh al-qamar (The moon's face) 66–8, 70, 144 n.15, *see also* female point of view
Wannūs, Sa'adAllāh 84–5
Wedding in Galilee (1987) 111
Wedeen, Lisa 10, 36, 101, 138 n.31
Weiss, Max 33, 90, 142 n.82
Western postmodernism 31
Westney, Emma 12
characters, categorization by 12
power-wielding characters 12
wielding power and stripped of power 12
women, *see also* female
dominant role of 112–13
objectification of 63
participation in public sphere 60
prominence and superiority 90
as repository of common sense 93–4
superiority 102–3
traits of ideal model 11

Yasin, Bū 'Ali 22
Yazbak, Samar 31, 34

Zhdanov, Andrei 18

www.ingramcontent.com/pod-product-compliance
Lightning Source LLC
Chambersburg PA
CBHW061839300426
44115CB00013B/2450
9780755644094